To Lis
with best wishes

Harry

BELOVED IMPERIALIST

SIR GORDON GUGGISBERG
GOVERNOR OF THE GOLD COAST

BELOVED IMPERIALIST

SIR GORDON GUGGISBERG
GOVERNOR OF THE GOLD COAST

by

H.B. Goodall

© H.B. Goodall 1998

First published in 1998 by
The Pentland Press Ltd.
1 Hutton Close
South Church
Bishop Auckland
Durham

British Library Cataloguing in Publication Data.
A catalogue record for this book is available
from the British Library.

ISBN 1 85821 557 9

Typeset by George Wishart & Associates, Whitley Bay.
Printed and bound by Bookcraft Ltd., Bath.

Dedication

This publication is dedicated to two of my Ghanaian friends, Professor W.N. (Bill) Laing and Dr T.D. (Tim) Osafo, men of great ability and warm friendliness, splendid ambassadors for their country.

Both were educated at Achimota College, the St Andrews University Medical Faculty (in St Andrews and Dundee) and the Royal Postgraduate Medical School, Hammersmith Hospital, London.

Professor Laing, who sadly died early this year, was head of pathology in the University of Ghana Medical School and was the first Dean of Medical Sciences at U.S.T. Kumasi.

Dr Osafo, now retired, was a clinical chemist at Korle-Bu Hospital (becoming an associate professor) and, more recently, in Sweden where he was a senior consultant and developed a large modern department of which he was head.

H.B.G.
Dundee, Scotland, UK
30 June 1997

Contents

List of Illustrations

Preface

This compact biography is a distillate of wide-ranging and patchily deep research on the life of Africa's most successful colonial governor – Sir Gordon Guggisberg. A gifted, brave and tenacious man, he is still a legend in Ghana, which, as the Gold Coast Colony, he administered from 1919 to 1927. He made substantial advances in transport, health and education and engendered an unsurpassed understanding and affection between ruler and ruled. He has largely been forgotten outside Ghana and this publication may, hopefully, help to resurrect the memory of someone who should not be allowed to slip into oblivion.

Acknowledgements

Special Acknowledgement
Sir Gordon Guggisberg is the hero of this biography. He is also, by his own words, a major contributor. So the book is partly an autobiography. Thus, almost seventy years since his death, he brings life to the narrative, with a voice denied him by his untimely passing. His part is acknowledged with deep gratitude.

Personal Acknowledgements
Mr A.H.M. Kirk-Greene, St Antony's College, Oxford, is warmly thanked for his friendly encouragement, expert advice and the wise guidance given in his Review *Towards a History of the Colonial Service* (African Affairs, 1974, Vol. 73, pp. 105 to 108).

The main burden of processing the script has been borne by Miss Gillian Bandeen, with skill, speed and cheerful enthusiasm; her efficiency has, thankfully, eased my load.

My wife, Jan, has had to endure, for years, my obsession with Guggisberg and has, from time to time, given sound advice; our son, Donald, has helped with his knowledge of German history.

Mr Hector Chawla FRCS gave me valuable comments in the early stage of writing. The vital boost to my researches on Sir Gordon came from an article and caricature in the *Nigerian Field*, loaned to me by the late Mr W. Halley Brown.

xiii

For helping to trace the management of that journal, I have to thank many people, especially Mr John Brown, the officers of Unilever Historical Archives, Dr (Mrs) Joyce Lowe (former Editor) and Dr (Mrs) Pat Oyelola (current Editor).

Research on Dr Burney's Royal Academy has been facilitated by Dr John Burston, Miss Angela K. Gill and Mr Ian Edelman.

The staffs of the Main and Medical Libraries, Dundee University have been most helpful. I am indebted for information related to the Royal Engineers to Captain 'Bob' Arnold, Mrs M. Magnusson and Sgt S. Cameron.

For guidance in the early stages of my researches I thank Professor A.D. Roberts, London, and Mr Higgins of the Foreign Office Library. Much of the basic research for this book has been done in the Public Record Office, Kew, and I am most appreciative of the help of its staff, especially Mr T.R. Padfield. Mr John Botwright, Cemeteries Officer, Bexhill-on-Sea, for information about Sir Gordon's funeral and grave.

My thanks go to the following in Ninewells Hospital and Medical School for their helpful co-operation: Professor D.A. Levison, Dr M. Faed, Dr A.J. Robertson, Mr S. McPherson, Mrs S. Gibb and Mrs M. Walker.

For the photographs of Sir Gordon Guggisberg's grave I am indebted to Mr John Hooper, Eastbourne. For other photographic support I thank I.N. Photo, Studio M and Prontaprint, both of Dundee. Fraulein Heidi Reisz, Swiss Centre, London, is kindly helping the search for the origin of the Guggisbergs. For use of the image of Burney's Academy I thank Gosport Museum.

I would also like to mention three special ladies: Mrs Gertrude Davies, whose father was Lt Col F.G. Guggisberg's chief clerk in Flanders; Mrs Nan Recordon, whose father was Comptroller of Customs in Accra; and Mrs Frances Radford, a former pupil of Achimota School – all three have been most helpful.

Finally, Mr Anthony Phillips, Mrs Mary Denton and their staff at Pentland Press have been efficient and friendly facilitators of this publication; they have very high standards.

Acknowledgements of Copyright and Permission
1: Those relating to illustrations are made with individual pictures in the text.
2: Those for quotations in the narrative (mainly in italics) are now appended in order of appearance.

Chapter III – almost all the material is out of Copyright. Cassells have raised no objection to the quoting of a few lines at the foot of page 11.

Chapter V – Permission Department of Thomas Nelson are unable to trace the records relating to *Modern Warfare*, but do not object to the use of material from the book.

Chapters VIII, IX, X and XI – all print in italics is from *We Two in West Africa* by Decima Moore and Major F.G. Guggisberg, by permission of William Heinemann.

Chapter XII – quotations in the script from the Southern Nigeria Survey have been cleared by the copyright officers of the Ordnance Survey who are concerned only with the copying of maps.

Chapter XVI – pp. 62 to 76 – the script in italics, copied

from Crown Copyright Material in the Public Record Office, Kew, is reproduced by permission of the Controller of Her Majesty's Stationery Office. Reference:- CO 96/608.21661 including 'covering letter' – CO 96/608.21661.54356, pp. 76–77 – comment by W.D. Ellis – CO 96/608.21661.54356, pp. 77–79 – letter from Guggisberg to Ellis – Ref. CO 96/608.21661.50552, p. 82 – telegram from Secretary of State to Governor of Gold Coast Colony – Ref. CO 96/608.21661.54356, p. 83 – Estimates in Report from Acting Governor (A.R. Slater), CO 96/608.45432.

Chapter XXII – p. 122. Paragraph re D.J. Oman from *Guggisberg* by R.E. Wraith is by courtesy of the Oxford University Press. pp. 127–41 – *The Keystone*, published by Simpkin, Marshall, Hamilton, Kent and Co. Ltd. London EC4. This firm's premises were completely destroyed with all their records in the Second World War. Thus no rights are traceable. (Information from Mr M. Bott, Reading University.)

Chapter XXIV

From the minutes of the Legislative Council meeting of 26 November 1919. Motion by Omanhene of Akim Abuakwa and seconded by Mr Brown. CO 98/33.15780.

This Crown Copyright Material in the Public Record Office, Kew, is reproduced by permission of the Controller of Her Majesty's Stationery Office.

Foreword

by

A.H.M. Kirk-Greene

Emeritus Fellow, St. Antony's College, Oxford.

Sir Gordon Guggisberg (1869–1930), who was Governor of the Gold Coast [Ghana since 1957] from 1919 to 1927, was a *rara avis* among Britain's 20th century colonial governors. In appearance every inch the classic colonial governor of common perception, tall, proud and distinguished, he was in fact anything but the typical Colonial Service governor. His life was, in the judgement of his hitherto sole biographer, Ronald Wraith, a constant paradox. Guggisberg was by profession a soldier and a surveyor, not a career colonial administrator. A convinced imperialist – though not a dyed-in-the-wool one – he is remembered in Ghana for having set the country on a better and faster course, in both infrastructural development and localization of the civil service, towards eventual independence than was the lot of any other African colony before 1939. Again, his personal conservatism was subordinated to the liberalism of his plans and policies for the Gold Coast, viewed by the Colonial Office as too far-reaching and too fast. Guggisberg was, too, one of the very few of Jewish descent ever to be appointed to a British colonial governorship. If his public service was a spectacular success, his private life was, as Dr Goodall concludes, a sorry failure. The strain of perpetual paradox running through Guggisberg's life is neatly encapsulated in Goodall's chosen title for his biographical study, 'Beloved Imperialist'.

Leaving aside Britain's final cadre of West African proconsuls when, like Sir John Macpherson and Sir James Robertson in Nigeria, Sir Charles Arden-Clarke in the Gold Coast and Sir Maurice Dorman in Sierra Leone, the last holder of the post was often a popular figure with the nationalist leadership and had indeed been purposely selected by the Colonial Office for his proven capacity to get on well with tomorrow's leaders, Guggisberg must rank, together with Sir Bernard Bourdillon in neighbouring Nigeria, as the most popular African governor of the inter-war years. His reputation lives on, seventy years after he left the splendid gubernatorial residence of Christiansborg Castle in Accra, as a positive modernizer and an empathetic ruler half a century ahead of his time. It is a measure of Ghanaians' genuine appreciation and affection that forty years after his death, and more than a decade into independence, at a time of widespread anti-colonial reaction when statues of Queen Victoria were being demolished or hidden away in urban rubbish-dumps all over the one-time Empire and nationalist legislatures were busy renaming the capital's streets after local heroes and no longer for passing proconsular personalities, the government of Ghana should initiate, commission and erect a statue to Sir Gordon Guggisberg. Today, Saka Acquaye's fine sculpture by the entrance to the teaching hospital in Accra reminds Ghanaians of Guggisberg's first material memorial to his governorship, that very same Korle-Bu Hospital which, founded in 1920, Guggisberg envisaged as a centre for medical training for the whole of West Africa.

In this new biographical study, Dr Goodall pays generous tribute to the pioneer biography of Guggisberg written by Ronald Wraith in 1967. In his account, Dr Goodall takes that admirable text three stages further. First, he uses archival material from Colonial Office files in the Public Record Office which was not accessible to Wraith thirty years ago. Secondly, to his interpretation of his subject he brings the inspiration and the interest of a professional medical man, not of an authority on public administration. Lastly, and arguably most importantly, Dr Goodall extends and enhances what is already known about Guggisberg's career by valuably scrutinizing each of Guggisberg's own, varied publications. These range from a rather juvenile and unsophisticated history of the Royal Military Academy at Woolwich (1900), through a much-praised technical survey report (1911) to the lighthearted and entertaining account by his wife and himself of their travels in up-country Gold Coast and Ashanti, *We Two in West Africa* (1909), culminating in two serious treatises on education, *The Keystone* (1924) and (with the Rev. A.G. Fraser) *The Future of the Negro* (1929).

Modestly reducing his own well-researched study to 'a distillate', Dr Goodall declares his aim as being not to smother the reader with blanket information but rather to stimulate him or her to ask, Oliver Twist-like, for more. In this he amply succeeds. His style is one of gentle presentation, not of aggressive argument or ideological appeal; indeed, it often recalls the comfortably relaxed style of the Guggisbergs' own *We Two in West Africa*. His biographical study is, if you like, a popularization of the man who was Guggisberg. At the same time, in his final chapter he takes scholarly issue with his predecessor biographer on a number of points of emphasis in the interpretation of Guggisberg's character and record. Nor is it the full story, for Dr Goodall promises us more to come, particularly on the implacable personality clash between Guggisberg and the aristocratic Sir Hugh Clifford, who regarded Guggisberg as 'a mountebank' and was mortified to learn that his successor as Governor of the Gold Coast was to be the very man whom he had earlier turned down for acceptance into the Colonial Service as his Chief Commissioner of the Northern Territories.

Dr Goodall's original anatomy of the Guggisberg *oeuvre* represents an interesting and helpful contribution to our knowledge and understanding of the life and work of Sir Gordon Guggisberg, the unusual colonial governor who, in his judgement, 'guided the Gold Coast to an enlightened and potentially prosperous future' and remains, seventy years on, 'a legend in Ghana'.

Oxford   A.H.M. Kirk-Greene
January 1998

Introduction

To many people nowadays the words *beloved* and *imperialist* would seem incompatible. Not so! For, if you visit the Municipal Cemetery at Bexhill-on-Sea, you will find a red granite headstone which shows that at least one imperialist, a colonial governor, was loved by those he ruled. The inscription reads:

TO THE EVERLASTING MEMORY OF
GOVERNOR SIR GORDON GUGGISBERG
WHO DIED IN 1930 AT BEXHILL.
THIS MEMORIAL WAS ERECTED BY THE
PARAMOUNT CHIEFS AND PEOPLE OF
THE GOLD COAST AND ASHANTI.

The circumstances in which this stone was erected are vividly described by R.E. Wraith in the final chapter of *Guggisberg*, the only detailed biography of this remarkable man. Wraith himself was an expert in African affairs and civil administration and published *Guggisberg* in 1967. It now seems appropriate to look again at Sir Gordon Guggisberg's life and give credit to at least one story of success in the face of the current inordinate criticisms of almost all matters imperial.

The unusual gravestone may have recorded the physical end of the man, but it can be used as the focus for the long-overdue resurrection of his name and fame to a deservedly high place in colonial history.

Sir Gordon Guggisberg governed the Gold Coast from 1919 to 1927. His administration was a material success, but, even more, he inspired all who worked with him, and won the admiration and affection of the peoples of the Gold Coast, Ashanti and their hinterland, the part of Africa now called Ghana. Guggisberg's unique leadership in the development of West Africa was the high plateau of activity and achievement in his life of devoted service.

The reader may well wonder how the writer, a medical teacher, first became interested in this outstanding man. In February 1971, I arrived in Accra as an external examiner and lecturer in the University of Ghana Medical School. The first morning in Accra I was driven to the front of the main teaching hospital – Korle-Bu Hospital – which was founded in 1920, later to become the focus for medical education. Beside the entrance is a statue. On enquiry, I was told that this was of Sir Gordon Guggisberg, the Governor who founded the hospital. The name Guggisberg seemed unusual for a British colonial administrator and I was told that he was a Canadian of partly Scottish, partly Jewish ancestry and that, before being appointed Governor of the Gold Coast, he had served as an officer in the Royal Engineers of the British Army.

I took a photograph to include the main entrance and the statue, but it was several years later that an article in the magazine, *Nigerian Field* really sparked my interest in Guggisberg; an interest which has become an obsession. I felt compelled to find out as much as I could about him and, hopefully, to pass on that knowledge to others. For his name has largely been forgotten, especially in Canada, the land of his birth. In fact the only group of people who really know about him are the former pupils of Achimota College near Accra (another of his major works).

Yet much has been written about his Governorship. He has a place in most historical accounts of West Africa. His career and character were succinctly but wonderfully portrayed in the Dictionary of National Biography by Lord (Sydney) Olivier (like Guggisberg an enlightened colonial administrator). The biography by R.E. Wraith was detailed, masterful and subtly humorous. Despite his exclusion from many relevant documents by the Government's fifty-year-rule, Wraith's 'personal memoir' is so thorough and shows such telling insight, that even with access to colonial records, an improvement on Wraith's *Guggisberg* would seem a difficult, if not impossible task (as was suggested in Canham's review of the book). (In African Affairs (1968) Vol 67, pp. 69–70.)

So why should an amateur be so bold as to write about Guggisberg? Mainly because so much has been forgotten. Let what follows be the justification!

Guggisberg was born in Toronto in 1869; he died at Bexhill-on-Sea in 1930. He was married twice, both times ultimately unhappily; there were three daughters from the first, two surviving to adult life; neither wed. He had three careers – military engineer, bush surveyor and colonial governor. He wrote several unusual books. His work took him to every continent but Australasia and Antarctica; thus he largely fulfilled the motto of the Royal Engineers – *Ubique!* I will prejudge this narrative by stating that, if a world-famous novelist had written the life of

Frederick Gordon Guggisberg as a work of fiction, it would have been hailed as his (or her) greatest book; it would today be on the shelves of every library. Yet the romantic reality of Wraith's scholarly work has been largely neglected. This must be redressed.

A large part of Wraith's book is concerned with Guggisberg's administration of the Gold Coast; and, after all, that encompassed his greatest material successes. Wraith himself had doubts about how substantial was the foundation on which his biography was based; in this he appears unnecessarily cautious. However, with the release of colonial office documents, a great deal of factual background is now available to supplement Wraith's work. We can now see a blow by blow account of Guggisberg's Governorship of the Gold Coast, from his controversial appointment by Lord Milner (an appointment detested by the professional colonial service), through his energetic and successful pursuit of plans for transport, health and, especially, education. Thus the full story can now be read of the construction of Takoradi harbour (with related rail and road developments), the building of Korle-Bu Hospital (the first major modern hospital in tropical Africa) and the founding of Prince of Wales (later Achimota) College, his flagship of African education. However, it is not the writer's intention to inflict total information of this type. The aim is to stimulate the reader to ask for more. This cannot be done with a surfeit of administrative details, engineering plans, contentious correspondence and political intrigues; it can only be done by portraying the man: a man of courage, dedicated to the service of the African; a professional engineer and surveyor, yet an undoubted romantic; a leader whose happy successes were achieved despite personal difficulties which must have made him sad.

The development of the powerful yet philanthropic character who excelled as Governor is the most fascinating aspect of the Guggisberg saga.

His personal papers disappeared during the Second World War and most people who knew him are dead. So the obvious sources of first-hand information have gone. But one does remain: the books he published. These have been used by others, but not to the full. It is thus the intention of this writer to trace the life of Gordon Guggisberg mainly through his own written words – the only way in which he himself can speak to us today. These books will serve as milestones on our way.[1]

---

1. Guggisberg's words from this page on are in italics.

Sir Gordon Guggisberg's grave.
The unique inscription reflects an amazing relationship. These
words helped to point the way to the title – Beloved Imperialist.
Photograph by John Hooper, Eastbourne.

Chapter I

ROOTS

'**W**hat's in a name?' In Guggisberg's case, much. To hear it for the first time is an auditory surprise; and, once heard, easily remembered. Because of anti-German feeling in Britain, Guggisberg may well have been uneasy about his surname, as in an incident at a formal dinner (recorded by Wraith). He was sitting beside a Lady Vischer, a cosmopolitan European. She leaned towards him and remarked, 'Guggisberg ... a good German name?'

'*Swiss, Madam,*' he corrected coldly, '*and the connection is very distant!*'

That closed the conversation and he turned somewhat abruptly to his other neighbour. (He must have been well aware how in 1914 Prince Louis of Battenberg was forced to resign from his post as First Sea Lord by anti-German hysteria and the family name changed to Mountbatten!)

Indeed Switzerland *was* the source of his name, specifically the village of Guggisberg, a little south of Bern, for a wedding in that small place started the family which, a century later and through almost unbelievable twists and turns of fate (or divine intervention), would produce a descendant who in eight momentous years would bring an under-developed African land into the modern world.

The bridegroom was a young Jewish glazier who had

1

wandered on foot from Eastern Poland to escape conscription in the Russian Army about the end of the eighteenth century; the bride was the daughter of a local German-Swiss market gardener who had employed the groom to work on his glasshouses. At first the father opposed the match, but, under pressure, it was allowed, provided that the groom became a Protestant and took the name of the village, Guggisberg, to help escape extradition. (This amazing story was told by Guggisberg during his final illness.)

The couple had two sons; both emigrated to Canada; the elder was Gordon Guggisberg's grandfather; he was a successful butcher and inn-keeper. The family prospered in Ontario, particularly in the manufacture of furniture, starting what became the 'Canadian Office and School Furniture Company'. The father of Gordon, Frederick by name, was recorded as being a successful 'inspector and dealer in dry goods' in the town of Galt.

In the normal course of events Guggisberg might have been expected to grow up in undistinguished prosperity in small-town Canada. But then came the first twist of fate – when he was four years old his father died.

Chapter II

TRANSPLANTATION

Guggisberg's mother, widowed, but comfortably off, moved to Toronto, where she met and married Paymaster RN Admiral Ramsey Dennis. (There were four daughters of this marriage, and three of them were wed to admirals!) The family moved to England when Guggisberg was ten years old. This move and the Senior Service connection had an important impact on his education, for, through his stepfather, he was enrolled in Dr Burney's Royal Academy, Gosport. Thus the boy from a humble family background in remote Continental Europe and Canada was almost spirited into the then largest and most famous private school in England and the only one under the immediate patronage of Queen Victoria. Many former pupils served with distinction in the Navy, Army and Indian Services and among them were the Duke of York (King George the Fifth) and Prince Louis of Battenberg (already mentioned). (What Gordon Guggisberg's American-born mother thought of this is not on record!)

This exclusive training ground for Imperial Service moved to Shalford House near Guildford in 1904, but by 1910 it had, perhaps surprisingly, fallen on evil days and become a hotel. Its records have disappeared, so Guggisberg's school performance cannot be examined. However, at least in its

PROSPECTUS
OF

THE ROYAL ACADEMY,

GOSPORT.

Patrons.

HER MOST GRACIOUS MAJESTY THE QUEEN.
HIS ROYAL HIGHNESS THE PRINCE OF WALES.
HIS ROYAL HIGHNESS THE DUKE OF EDINBURGH.

In this Establishment, YOUNG GENTLEMEN are educated for the Navy, Army, the Civil Service,
the Learned Professions, Public Schools, &c.,

BY

THE REV. EDWARD BURNEY, M.A.,

E. L. SHEWELL, M.A., VICE-PRINCIPAL.

THE TERMS ARE FIFTY GUINEAS A YEAR FOR PUPILS UNDER 16 YEARS OF AGE
SIXTY GUINEAS A YEAR FOR PUPILS OVER 16 YEARS OF AGE,

WHICH INCLUDE

EVERY BRANCH OF A SOUND CLASSICAL AND ENGLISH EDUCATION.

THE FOLLOWING ARE EXTRA CHARGES: — *German, French, Drawing, Steam, Fortification, Geometrical Drawing, each One Guinea a Quarter. Boating with Bathing, and Gymnastics, each Half a Guinea a Quarter. Paper, Pens, Ink, Desk, and a Seat in the Church, Half a Guinea a Quarter. Washing, One Guinea a Quarter.*

This School was established in the year 1791, by the late Dr. W. Burney, and was for many years honoured by the immediate patronage of his late Most Gracious Majesty King William the Fourth; His Royal Highness the much lamented Prince Consort was also its Patron. The Plan of Education is liberal and comprehensive, great attention is paid to the study of Modern Languages, of which there are two Professors.

The Establishment is of large extent, and eligibly situated in a fine open square, opposite the Dock Yard, and adjoining Portsmouth Harbour; its situation offers many advantages to Military as well as to Naval Pupils.

Four Fourteen-oared Boats are kept for the use of the Pupils, who have the advantage of Sea-bathing and of learning to Swim; they are always accompanied by the Masters and experienced Boatmen.

The School Room and Class Rooms are large and convenient; there is a select Library; an extensive Play-ground, and a Field. The strictest attention is paid to the domestic treatment of the Pupils, and every arrangement is made to promote their health and comfort.

The Vacations are Six Weeks at Midsummer, the same at Christmas, commencing about the 16th of June, and the 16th of December, during which, when special preparation is required for an examination, the charge is Three Guineas a week.

The Young Gentlemen on joining the Academy are to bring not less than Two Suits of Clothes, a Great Coat, Ten Shirts, Four Night Shirts, Eight pairs of Cotton and Six pairs of Worsted Stockings, Three pairs of Boots or Shoes, Six Pocket-handkerchiefs, Six Towels, and a set of Combs and Brushes, a Silver Fork and Spoon, all plainly marked. They are allowed Sixpence weekly for pocket-money, until they are Twelve Years of Age, when (with the sanction of their Friends) they can have a Shilling.

It is particularly requested that the Pupils return to School as punctually as possible at the termination of each Vacation; also, that they should not join with a larger sum of money than *One Guinea*.

The Accounts are made up at Midsummer and Christmas, and are expected to be discharged in the course of the Vacation, or when the Young Gentlemen return to School.

N.B.—A Quarter's Notice, or payment, is required on removing a Pupil, unless to the Military Colleges, or into the Navy or Army.

₀ *Gentlemen are thoroughly prepared for all the competitive Examinations for direct Commissions in the Army; they also go with many advantages from this Establishment into the Royal Navy, and are expeditiously qualified for the Royal Military College at Sandhurst, for Woolwich, for the Royal Marines, for the Civil Service, and the Steam and Mercantile Marine Services.*

₀ Pupils joining for Special Preparation, after having received their nominations to the Navy or Marines, are charged Ten Guineas a Month.

Guggisberg's 'Old School'. A fascinating prospectus!
It is interesting that two of the extra subjects offered, Fortification
and Geometrical Drawing, were the subjects taught by Guggisberg
at the Royal Military Academy – did he first study them at
Dr Burney's Royal Academy?
Reproduced by kind permission of the Hampshire County
Council Museums Service (original in Gosport Museum).

Gosport days, it had a high reputation and surely the character-building element of Governor Guggisberg's plans for education of the African must have been derived from the strict Anglican traditions of Dr Burney's establishment.

The next stage of Guggisberg's education was at the Royal Military Academy, Woolwich, from 1886 to 1889 and he must have been enthused by life in the organization, because he was later appointed an Instructor there in Fortification and Geometrical Drawing (1897) and wrote its history in *The Shop: the Story of the Royal Military Academy*. Although the book was not published until 1900 and much happened in his life before that, it is appropriate to consider this, his first major publication, now, because it reflects his cadetship at the RMA and gives clues to his character, interests and potential.

Guggisberg's 'Old School'. An imposing building!
Reproduced by kind permission of the Hampshire County Council Museums Service
(original in Gosport Museum).

Chapter III

THE SHOP: THE STORY OF THE ROYAL MILITARY ACADEMY

This book shows that Guggisberg had an intense interest in and devotion to his alma mater: enough to record much of his personal experiences and to do detailed research on historical documents of the Academy. Professional historians may have looked upon it as a slightly naive record by an inexperienced writer, but it has much to recommend it. The fact that every detail is there is both a strength and a weakness. Yet it must have increased the public's awareness of how 'gunner' and 'sapper' officers of the British Army were chosen and trained and what sort of characters they really were.

Guggisberg's research material spanned from 1741 to 1900; and he goes about it in the manner of a military engineer, surveying the scene and defining positions at successive stages; all done with the thoroughness which was his hallmark in later life.

The first words of the book are '*When was the Academy started?*' (No vague general preliminaries!) There had been arguments about the date and manner of its inception, but he was sure.

Royal Military Academy. An early picture. The Warren and Rupert's Tower.
(From *The Shop – the Story of the Royal Military Academy*, 1900, Cassell and Co., London.)

We have no less an authority than that of His Majesty King George the Second for fixing [exact co-ordinates!?] *upon the 30th of April 1741 as the right and proper date. Here are the words of the Royal Warrant signed on that day; the word* <u>instituted</u> *seems to leave no room for doubt:-*

'George R.,

Whereas you, our right and trusty and right entirely beloved Cousin and Councillor, John, Duke of Montagu, Master General of our Ordnance, hath laid before us a representation . . . that it would conduce to the good of our service if an Academy or School was <u>instituted,</u> *endowed and supported, for instructing the raw and inexperienced people belonging to the Military Branch of this office, in the several parts of Mathematics necessary to qualify them for the service of the Artillery and the business of Engineers; and that there is a convenient room at Woolwich Warren, which is our property, and may be fitted up for that purpose; we having taken the subject into out Royal consideration, and approving thereof our will and pleasure is that we do hereby authorise, empower and direct you to nominate, constitute, and appoint an able and skilfull Master and Assistants, and to prescribe such Rules, Orders, and Regulations, from time to time, as you shall think fit and expedient for the instruction and improvement of the people, and for the good government of the said Academy or School; . . . etc. etc.'*

The Master General lost no time in issuing 'Rules and Orders for the Royal Academy at Woolwich' and the work of the school started at the end of the year (1741) in the said Woolwich Warren, a house close to a mansion once the residence of Prince Rupert. We can thus see the thoroughness of Guggisberg's research and writing; but there is no need to emulate him in the relentless recording of detail. So, for the sake of brevity, we will continue to look at

'The Shop' in a series of episodes and notes of particular interest.

We hear much nowadays about the indiscipline and rebellion of youth, but here is an eye-opening letter home from a Mr R. Sandham, a cadet at the Academy in 1750:

> *I suppose, Mamma, you are desirous of knowing what acquaintance I have commenced during the short time I have been at Woolwich. I believe I need not inform you of the caution that is required in choosing an intimacy among a set of young fellows whose most honourable epithet is* wild. *The generality of them bear the worst of characters, being ever engaged in riots and drunken broils, in one of which a lieutenant . . . was lately wounded and lost the use of his middle finger; he lodges in the same house with me.*

In these early days, cadets were lodged in *reputable* houses in the Woolwich area, the School not yet having living-in accommodation. Guggisberg comments: *'Sandham's letters, priggish though they may be, give us a life-like picture of 'The Shop' of those days . . . The roughest kind of practical joking and a fiendish kind of bullying were the favourite amusements.'* Many of these activities appear to have been shared with young officers already commissioned.

To turn to more academic affairs it must have been a nightmare for masters to teach such a disparate group of youths – ranging widely in age, ability and previous experience of mathematical subjects. Once living accommodation in the Academy was available there must have been administrative chaos with resident, fully enrolled Gentlemen Cadets – GC; some enrolled but awaiting lodging vacancies (Extra Cadets) and others more loosely attached,

10

so-called <u>Gentlemen Attendants</u>. In his usual detailed way Guggisberg gives the full menu for the feeding of the hungry young men, the precise fare for each day of the week and for special occasions.

About the beginning of the nineteenth century a pernicious form of bullying had to be stamped out by the Lieutenant-Governor (LG), the officer in military command of the cadets (as distinct from the senior master). Thus in 1810, the LG gave notice that he would severely punish those whose *'object . . . is to impede the progress of those Cadets, who were keen to advance their knowledge'*. (Idle characters trying to spread idleness by savage bullying.) One problem was that some of the troublemakers had wealthy, influential parents.

By Guggisberg's time as a cadet great improvements had been made. There still was a spartan regime, e.g. cold baths every morning throughout the year, but dining facilities were improved, with a substantial dinner in the evening, not just a late tea with bread and cheese. The introduction of sporting activities – athletics, football and especially cricket – channelled energy and aggression. Dancing classes were part of the curriculum and formal dances with appropriate young ladies were held.

In quaintly romantic, adolescent language, Guggisberg describes such a social occasion: *'The gym is transformed into a veritable palace of delight where the fairy slippers of the beauteous maiden and the glossy wellingtons of the bold gentleman cadet glide smoothly over the well-polished floor to the dulcet strains of the gunners band.'* Young Gordon was obviously susceptible to the charms of lovely girls; and they found him similarly attractive, for by then he had grown into a very tall, athletic, elegant and extraordinarily handsome beau – a potentially explosive mixture, soon to be ignited.

Cricket was his other great passion and 'The Shop' contains every detail of thirty-three matches between the Royal Military Academy, Woolwich and the Royal Military College, Sandhurst; not just the scores in every innings, but bowling averages, highest scores and other statistics. Of the 33 matches, Woolwich won 9, Sandhurst 15 and 9 were drawn. Guggisberg became a member of the MCC (playing when time permitted) and of other fashionable clubs, whose ties he liked to sport. As we shall see, he continued as an active cricketer after being commissioned.

'The Shop' shows that Gordon Guggisberg was endowed with singleness of purpose, mental stamina and the ability to handle a large amount of detail. In those days before the burgeoning of information technology, men like him were at a premium, for he had an almost computer-like mind. His enthusiasms and romantic tendencies, too, were emerging as vital factors in his career.

Chapter IV

'SOMEWHERE EAST OF SUEZ'

In 1889 Guggisberg was gazetted 2nd Lieutenant in the Royal Engineers. In 1893 he was promoted Lieutenant and posted to Singapore, where he was in charge of the Local (Malay) Submarine Mining Company. He worked hard and played hard. He was by now an accomplished batsman and bowler and with a fellow sapper became the mainstay of the Straits Settlements Cricket Team, which competed with teams from Hong Kong and Shanghai. So he must have spent a considerable time on board ship between these outposts of the Empire. By dint of school, college, military service and sporting prowess the young Canadian was by now well integrated with the English ruling class.

Guggisberg was highly popular with the ladies, although, according to Wraith, the flirtations appeared to be 'innocent enough'. But then, in 1895, it happened: he fell madly in love with his commanding officer's daughter (Ethel Emily Hamilton Way, daughter of Colonel Wilfred Way RE). She reciprocated; she was only seventeen, beautiful, fair-haired, but inexperienced in both romantic and domestic affairs. The colonel opposed their wish to get married (remember a similar episode a hundred years before in the village of Guggisberg!), but encouraged by her more romantically

13

inclined mother, they eloped to Colombo, were married and spent their honeymoon on Ceylon.

It is fascinating that at the same time that Gordon Guggisberg was in Malaya, his predecessor as Governor of the Gold Coast, Hugh Clifford, was also there. While Guggisberg was still a somewhat reckless junior army officer, Clifford was already established as a colonial administrator, diplomat and military leader. As far as the writer is aware, there is no published record of their paths having crossed 'East of Suez', but did they and did their long antipathy, stronger on Clifford's side, start in the Orient?

In 1896 Guggisberg was posted back to Britain and next year was appointed Instructor in Fortification and Geometrical Drawing at the RMA. Back at Woolwich he had a distinguished career, reforming the syllabus and methods of instruction (a born teacher) and writing *The Shop* which we have already considered.

Three daughters were born of the hasty marriage; the first died in infancy. The union gradually disintegrated. Despite his earnest instructions, his wife was incapable of running a home on his limited income and disaster finally struck when he got his mother to take charge of the domestic situation! Ethel, a girl of spirit, responded to that insult by running away with an Anglican parson. Guggisberg divorced her in 1904.

His domestic problems did not appear to interfere with his teaching and writing and in 1903 he published, under the pseudonym 'Ubique', an extraordinary book *Modern Warfare*.

Chapter V

MODERN WARFARE

This book was written primarily to instruct a young
relative about the form and functions of the British
Army. Of its five hundred pages, the first seventy detail the
various types of unit, the personnel making up these units
and how they are integrated into large battle formations,
particularly an army corps in the field. A copy of
Guggisberg's own hand-printed diagram of the structure of
such a corps (the British First Corps) tells more than many
pages of script.

Where mobility was needed, a corps (usually of over
35,000 men) was often supplemented by a cavalry division.
In those days a general commanded the corps and a
lieutenant general each division. Although Guggisberg was
only a captain (gazetted 1900), he obviously had a detailed
knowledge of the functions of officers of higher rank and not
just of engineers. He conveys also the romantic side of
soldiering, but contrasts the smartly turned out, colourful,
confident troops on a sovereign's review with the shattered
survivors of a South African siege. (Guggisberg did not serve
in the Boer War, but, only a year after it ended, he, like
soldiers and civilians generally, still felt its warning shock to
the mighty Empire.)

However, the fascinating and major part of *Modern Warfare*

The First Corps of the British Army. Details so typical of Guggisberg's all-inclusive style!
(From *Modern Warfare*, 1903, Thomas Nelson and Sons Ltd.)

16

is a fictional, yet precisely detailed description of a campaign in Belgium, waged by the First Corps of the British Army against the Germans. The story has many similarities to what actually happened eleven years later and, after studying Guggisberg's words, we will consider the possible significance of the uncanny *déjà vu.*

Here is how he describes the build-up to the campaign:

'In the month of May, nearly thirty-five years after the great war between France and Germany in 1870, it is evident to the whole world that the two great military nations are again preparing to fight each other.

Eventually war is declared, and on the 15th of June over 350,000 German troops cross the boundary and invade France between Nancy and Belfort.' A stalemate appears to be developing, with French reserves mobilized to stiffen resistance. *'What eventually happens is that nearly all the best trained troops in France are drawn towards Belfort.* [South-East]. *Then suddenly, a German army of over 200,000 men crosses the frontier of Belgium . . . in order to cut across the rear of the French armies and advance on Paris.'* By an agreement of 1831, Britain is obliged to resist the Germans (and indeed any other power's invasion of Belgium) and thus Britain and Germany are at war.

Guggisberg then describes in detail the process of mobilization of the First Army Corps preparatory to going to the aid of the Belgians whose army is no match for the Germans. His details range from decisions of the high command to personal points about individual units and even individual soldiers being recalled from leave. He seems to have had a particular 'attachment' to the First Royal Dublin

Fusiliers and the 2nd Gordon Highlanders.[1] As in the real war in 1914, General John French is appointed to command the British Expeditionary Force!

With his imaginative, total overview of the situation Guggisberg argues the case for using Ostend as the main landing and supply port. Nothing escapes his attention: e.g. *'The Army Veterinary Department establishes a large Horse Hospital at Ostend ... This is a very necessary precaution, for in a couple of weeks of warfare nearly half the horses of an army are disabled in some way or other.'* Nor does he forget the Royal Yacht's part in the sailing of the force from the Thames. *'The Royal Standard floats from the Yacht's masthead over two persons standing on the bridge, one in the brilliant scarlet uniform of a British Field-Marshal, the other a slender willowy figure in a graceful clinging black dress. They are the King and Queen – God bless them! – come to wish their army Godspeed!'*

But now to the real fighting south of Brussels. Chapter XXIV is entitled 'THE IRISH BRIGADE AT WORK' and is introduced thus:

> *A letter from Lieutenant Daniel Brady of B Company Royal Dublin Fusiliers, to his brother at Wellington College, in which he describes how the Irish Brigade fortified Hutte Wood.*
>
> *My dear Tim, – You will be playing Charterhouse today. Good luck to you and the old school. I hope you will beat them.*
>
> *Bedad, old man, you'll have to try to get into Sandhurst next exam. Fighting is hard work, but it is splendid for all that, provided you don't get hit. But you have to take your chance of that. You ought to have no difficulty in getting a commission in the* Dear Dirty Dublins, *for there will be plenty of vacancies in the regiment*

---

1. He may have been attracted by the name of the latter, but why the former?

*before this war is over, bad luck to it. There's many a good fellow
gone already.*

Such was the pace and confusion of the conflict that even to
read the 28-page letter is tiring! Perhaps surprisingly there is
no indication of censorship. The carnage was horrific,
especially among the Germans, who were attacking in the
face of the then new Lee-Enfield rifle. A wet, chilly night
brings a respite, but not for long. *'The bloody twentieth century
battle of Waterloo is about to begin.'*

This final battle is best shown by Guggisberg's free-hand
map. (Map 15); the alternative of over sixty pages of
description is just too much! An area of only 7 by 5 miles is
packed with tens of thousands of troops in terrain offering
only scant defensive cover. Little wonder that the British
lose 12,000 killed and wounded out of 35,000 men; the
Germans 41,000 out of 110,000! The smaller British remnant
is vulnerable to further assault, but help is at hand. General
French receives a telegram.

'I expect to reach HAL [presumably the town of Halle, south-
west of Brussels] *at eight o'clock tomorrow evening with the 2nd
and 3rd Army Corps. Hold on to your positions at all costs.*
KITCHENER.'

*When the sun rises on the 21st of July its rays flash on the German
Army in full retreat ... unable to withstand the attack of 70,000
fresh opponents ... the battle is over!*

At this stage in his life, Guggisberg's genius for imaginative, meticulous detail contrasts with his apparently
irresponsible, almost puerile attitude to the grim realities of

19

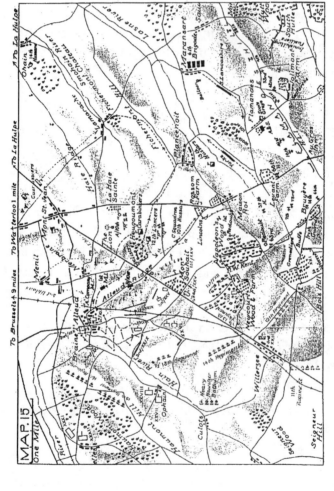

The Twentieth-Century Battle of Waterloo. This again shows the amazing ability of Guggisberg to deal with complex details. One interesting aspect is the more 'homely' names of British units, contrasting with the merely numbered German formations. (From *Modern Warfare*, 1903, Thomas Nelson and Sons Ltd.)

20

war (even given the fact that he was writing for a young person). Two further major experiences were yet to contribute to the development of the mature, devoted governor – bush surveying in West Africa and active service on the Western Front.

However, before going forward to these fields of fresh endeavour, one feels compelled to look briefly at the almost prophetic nature of *Modern Warfare*.

Chapter VI

MODERN WARFARE AND THE SCHLIEFFEN PLAN

*M*odern Warfare was published in 1903, the Schlieffen Plan in 1905-6. The latter was a memorandum by Count Alfred von Schlieffen, Chief of Staff of the German Army, setting out guidelines for fighting a war on two fronts against the French and the Russians and including a plan to attack France through Belgium. Did Guggisberg's book play any part in suggesting such a move? Indeed Wraith notes that the book 'was commended by Marshal Oyama of Japan and other distinguished soldiers'. I investigated the possibility in several publications about the start of the First World War and found that it was much more likely that the idea of a strong outflanking attack by the right wing of the German Army was based not on Guggisberg's fictitious campaign of *two years before*, but on Hannibal's tactics at the historic Battle of Cannae *two thousand years before*! Apparently German staff officers were indoctrinated in the tactics of that famous victory.[1] It was fortunate for the Allies in 1914 that the German General Staff, headed then by Helmut von Moltke (nephew of the famous nineteenth-century general), fearful of the strength of the Tsar's army, moved four of the

---

1. The American masterplan for the recent Gulf War was also based on that ancient battle.

eleven divisions earmarked for the Belgian campaign to the Eastern Front and so weakened their thrust towards Paris that they failed to break through. Other possibilities are that Guggisberg had some prior knowledge of the Schlieffen Plan or that he himself had thought of it independently and flew a personal kite to alert Allied military staff. Amazingly the French were either ignorant of or ignored the warnings! Finally, when Guggisberg saw the carnage of Flanders and thought of his light-hearted story did this contribute to his later dedication to good works?

Chapter VII

SURVEYING IN WEST AFRICA

In 1902 Guggisberg was seconded from the Royal Engineers and employed under the Colonial Office on a special survey of the Gold Coast and Ashanti. In those days such an arrangement was not uncommonly used to relieve a difficult marital situation, but there was also a pressing need for the survey, because the scramble for gold-prospecting concessions had precipitated a chaotic situation in the many areas which were as yet unmapped. Gordon Guggisberg, with his flair for detail and drawing, was an ideal choice for the task. This was indeed the major turn of fate in the making of the great colonial leader.

It is appropriate here to pay tribute also to an earlier surveyor, George Ekem Ferguson, a native of the Gold Coast, who was one of the first of his compatriots to receive advanced education and, after secondary schooling in Freetown, was trained in Britain as a surveyor. As well as surveying, he acted as a government agent, concluding treaties with various tribes. His murder in 1897 at Wa, in the Northern Territory, deprived the Colony of one of its most able pioneers. No doubt Guggisberg knew of this gifted man, who also is still revered in Ghana.

It is interesting that the Governor of the Gold Coast appointed in 1900, Sir Matthew Nathan, was a Royal

Engineer and it was he who ordered the special survey to implement the so-called Concession Ordinance. A fellow sapper, Major Alan Watherston, who had previously been in charge of surveys in Nigeria, was appointed Director and Guggisberg Assistant Director (he later succeeded Watherston as Director).

Guggisberg quickly warmed to the task. With a team of sappers and local labourers and porters he systematically surveyed great tracts of scarcely passable virgin forest. The field work was done in the dry season, from October to May. The term 'dry' in that part of Africa is not a strict one, for, even during these months, severe thunderstorms with torrential downpours may occur. Living conditions under canvas and the protection of instruments and records must have been difficult, in the dust of the harmattan as well as in the rain. But the dedicated Guggisberg completed each year's work and prepared reports and maps while back in Britain, his only relaxation being during the ocean voyage home.

Two books developed from Guggisberg's surveying activities and they will provide details.

Chapter VIII

WE TWO IN WEST AFRICA

This book was published in 1909 under the joint authorship of Decima Moore and Major F.G. Guggisberg. Someone else was on centre stage! And in more ways than one, for, a year after he divorced Ethel Emily, he married Lilian Decima, a leading musical comedy actress. She starred with the D'Oyly Carte Opera Company, particularly in the Second Soprano Part of Casilda in *The Gondoliers* – Miss Decima Moore was reported as looking quite bewitching in one of the new fashionable capes. Even in her second flush of youth (she had already been married) she certainly bewitched the bold Gordon, and, presumably, he her. Romance and drama were never far away! As divorcees they were married in a register office; Decima's sister Ada was bridesmaid and Arthur Conan Doyle (a cricketing buddy) best man!

Thus, in subsequent sojourns in Africa, he was accompanied by this attractive, yet formidable lady.

But, even in the Preface to their book, a substantial, illustrated account of their travels in the Gold Coast and Ashanti, he already expresses annoyance with his new wife virtually on their honeymoon!

The Preface runs thus:

This is a most irritating book to read. My wife wanted to write an account of her travels – I wanted to write an account of mine. My wife was a newcomer and saw the novelty of things – I was a fairly old inhabitant and had grown accustomed to living in strange surroundings. My wife kept notes – I did not. The book in fact may either be described as experience looking on things through new glasses, or as a fresh receptive mind regarding the 'Coast' with the eyes of experience.

What makes our book additionally irritating is that, whenever we arrive at a by-path we unhesitatingly go down it. The slightest excuse, in fact, makes us ramble miles from the subject in hand at the moment.

Throughout the book my wife talks – I write.

F.G.G.

The book is not just a travelogue; it is a unique commentary on the West African colonial scene. The Guggisbergs were enterprising pioneers and Decima was the first European woman to visit some of the remote areas. They had to be self-reliant, even in their own medical care. But let them do the talking!

Even the voyage from Liverpool sets the scene:

It was in the evening of I think the third day after leaving Grand Canary that I first made my acquaintance with the 'Coast', although we were many hundred miles from our destination . . . our boat was steaming steadily along through a perfectly calm sea, and all around were the sounds of shipboard life . . . Suddenly I noticed one of my companions, an old 'Coaster', lean forward, sniff violently at the air, and then lie back in his chair with an expression that was almost ecstatic. Before I had time to inquire the reason of this, another man ejaculated, 'By jove, it is . . .' (Sniff, sniff).

27

'You're right,' growled a third, promptly rising and making for the companion way. 'Hold on,' said a fourth, 'I'll come too,' and he also bolted. 'What is the matter with you all?' I asked turning to my husband, only to find him also sniffing the air. 'The smell of the Coast,' he replied. 'Don't you notice it? Those two are rather nervous and have gone for their quinine.'

The Smell of the Coast. It is not a pretty phrase, nor is it very accurate, but it is certainly expressive of the strange mixture of smell and feel with which the land wind is laden. It is damp and clammy and cool – you can taste it on your lips and in your nostrils there comes just a suspicion of forests and swamps and rank vegetation. But the whole effect is indescribable – it is a mental more than a physical feeling.

(In fact the land wind is dangerous, for it can carry potentially infectious malarial mosquitos out to sea. Some of the earliest experiences of this writer with patients suffering from malaria were with men of the Merchant Navy who had sailed from Cape Town to Britain along the coast of West Africa, but never set foot on its shores.)

Chapter IX

LANDING THROUGH THE SURF

The final stages of the Guggisbergs' voyage to the Gold Coast (Decima's first) ended with dramatic landings in open boats through the surf; first at Sekondi and then at Accra. Indeed these episodes serve to highlight one of the major facts of life (and occasionally death) for travellers to that shore before the construction of the deep-water harbour at Sekondi (Takoradi) and that it was Guggisberg himself who provided the drive and organizing ability to make a reality of the dream project.

Their landing first at Sekondi was to supervise the setting out of the season's surveying teams from that town, in which was the ocean end of the railway. (The initial landings in lighters and barges of rails and rolling stock must in themselves have been feats of engineering!).

Their ship, the *Mendi*, on her maiden voyage, anchored two miles offshore and was met by a flotilla of small craft to ferry passengers, baggage, mail and cargo to the beach.

The gangway ladder can very seldom be lowered and was not on this occasion, as the boats were rising and falling eight to ten feet alongside.

The Guggisbergs were lowered from a derrick into a small mail-boat for the landing.

We sat on basket-chairs near the stern of the boat, the mail-bags piled in the middle. In the bow waved the blue ensign from a small staff. In the stern on a small deck flush with the gunwhales stood the coxswain, steering with a long oar thrust through a grummet of rope. Our crew of ten men in blue jerseys and knee-breeches were perched on the gunwhales much as a woman sits a horse, facing forward, the big toe of one foot holding on to a loop of rope attached to the inner side of the boat, and the toes of the other gripping the ribs and thwarts . . . Magnificent men they were, and, when presently they took their jerseys off it was superb to see the muscles swelling and rippling along their ebony backs as they leant far out over the sides of the boat and plunged their paddles with a tchunk into the water, keeping the most perfect time.

The dangerous part was close to the beach where the rollers broke into foaming surf on rocks and sand bars.

Just before approaching this the paddles slowed down and the boat swung lazily forward, while the steersman, casting glances astern over his shoulder, selected a favourable moment for rushing the dangerous spot. Looking out to sea he was able with his long experience to gauge the size of the rollers, and, at the crucial moment, after a wait of several minutes, he gave the signal. With wild shouts and stamps of his foot he urged on his crew; the latter leant forward and outward, dug their paddles into the water, and burst into a weird song. A big roller came up astern, caught the boat and urged her forward with lightning speed until it passed away in front leaving us in a hollow. Then the song gradually died away and changed to a strange sort of hissing sound as the men, paddling furiously drew breath through their clenched teeth. With almost superhuman effort they prevented the surf-boat from being sucked back by the undertow until just as it seemed as if their efforts would be unavailing, the wild chant broke out and again the boat dashed madly forward until, the dangerous moment over, the paddlers relaxed their efforts, and we

Fishing near Tema – March 1971. Surf boats, similar to those which landed Gordon and Decima Guggisberg ninety years ago are still used for inshore fishing. From some vantage points along the coast one could see, far out on the horizon, the superstructures of Eastern Bloc factory fishing ships doing their utmost to empty the ocean to provide fish manure for Communist Europe!

glided into the comparative calm . . . behind the reef . . . Exactly what might have happened if we upset?

We Two conveys an exciting sense of wonder and adventure and a liberal and balanced view of the relative merits of African and European cultures and technologies. One fascinating remark was how the result of the Battle of Omdurman, nearly 3,000 miles away, had travelled by 'bush telegraph' more rapidly to West Africa than to London! Both husband and wife appeared genuinely interested in the people of the 'Coast' and this was a big factor in their acceptance as leaders a decade later.

But let's get down to the business of surveying. Accra was the actual headquarters of the survey, but, as already mentioned, most teams started from Sekondi, as many of them travelled by train to where they were to start work. A Captain Symons RE, and assistants, had arrived a week before with most of the equipment, which they had already organized for the teams. A heap for each comprised: *'valuable theodolites in leather cases, steel tapes, banderoles with gay little flags, compasses, axes, hatchets, saws, spades, tents, cooking pots, beds, basins, baths, blotting-paper, writing-paper, paints, pens, pencils, drawing-paper, plan cases, india-rubber, sealing-wax, ink, sun-umbrellas, tropical raincoats, pith helmets, books'.* All had to be in good order, complete and accessible when required. Each team had a lengthy memorandum on their plans and duties and money to pay carriers and for other purposes.

'The staff was divided into ten parties, each consisting of two or three Europeans with their boys and cooks, and interpreter, a couple of native policemen, and about fifty carriers in two gangs.' Stores were packed into loads of 56 to 60lb suitable for carrying on the bearers' heads, the contents of every package being recorded. It all appeared a very impressive feat of organization.

The Guggisbergs moved on by the next ship to Accra and endured an even rougher landing than at Sekondi. One boat overturned; five had done so a week before, when Major Guggisberg's polo pony was disembarked. Sadly the officer who accomplished this difficult manoeuvre, a Captain Stoddart, lately of the Royal Artillery, died soon after of blackwater fever.

The main landing problem at Accra was that the last

hundred yards or so of a boat's course was parallel to the beach and thus water was often shipped, sometimes with disastrous consequences, but entertaining to spectators on shore. The leading coxswain at Accra, the one-eyed, so-called 'Tin Eye' also saw the funny side of landing terrified, first-time travellers.

Life was a little less exciting just east of Accra in the area of Christiansborg Castle, the seat of government – still unpredictably hazardous, but not unlike similar postings in other remote parts of the Empire.

Chapter X

TRAVELS WITH THE SURVEY TEAMS

A s with the other books we must of necessity sample only a few of the many experiences recorded. The travellers were occasionally on trains, sometimes on passable roads of red (laterite) earth, but often through difficult forest tracks. When the going was tough, Decima had an unusual form of transport – a hammock, sometimes a sitting-hammock, but more often a lying-hammock.

The lying-hammock is made of a 7-foot length of canvas, which is kept stretched broadways by two curved pieces of wood, one at each end. These are suspended from hooks at the end of a stout bamboo rod, about 12 feet long, roughly lashed at right angles to two short boards which rest on the four hammock-boys, heads. The hammock, naturally sags in the middle, and unless you put a cushion under your knees you soon develop a pain in the back of your legs and numbness in your heels.

The boys walk in pairs beside each other, two at the head and two at the foot. They use pads on their heads, a piece of native cloth rolled up like a turban, and carry you along at a fast walk, often breaking into a jog-trot, swinging arms with a curious loose motion of the shoulders and only putting their hands to steady it when they come to some place where the going is treacherous . . . Each man walks out of step with his neighbour, for, if all walk in step, as occasionally happens for a moment, you get severely shaken and swing to and fro in a manner most upsetting to your interior. When nearing home they often break into a fast run of seven or eight miles an hour. There is no surer barometer to the state of their feelings than the pace at which they carry you.

Usually the hammock-passenger was carried feet first; but positions were reversed when climbing up steep hills. Visibility tended to be rather restricted.

An unusual form of hammock, a bullet-proof hammock was used to carry Lady Hodgson – the wife of Sir Frederick Hodgson, a previous Governor of the Gold Coast – in a column escaping from the siege of Kumasi Fort only a few years before the Guggisbergs' safari.

The map at the back of the book shows the places visited. They went by train to Tarkwa, where they saw two disparate aspects of development – the goldmines and the botanical gardens, the former commercial successes, but scars on the landscape, the latter a centre for developing crops for local consumption and commerce, all described by *We Two* in a very enlightened way. They showed disquiet with the more ruthless aspects of the gold trade and advocated the need for genuine planning of mining activities. The Europeans employed by the mining companies appeared rather inferior citizens compared with those in government work. Decima certainly disapproved of the olfactory results of the miners' less than adequate personal hygiene; on the other hand she praised the bathing habits of the Africans. Their train journey then took them to Dankwa, Obuasi and finally Kumasi where they spent a week preparing for further exploration.

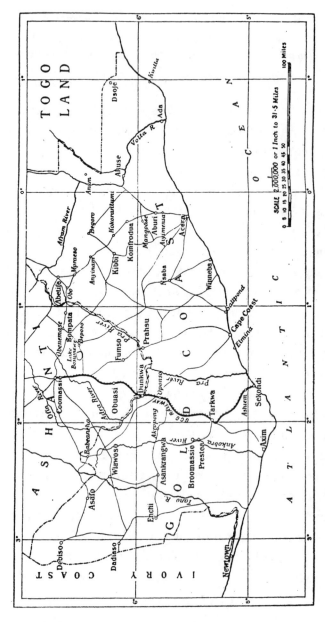

The Gold Coast – Map drawn at the time of Guggisberg's surveying work.
(From *We Two in West Africa*; permission of William Heinemann.)

36

They stayed at the Fort of Kumasi as guests of Mr Francis Fuller, the Chief Commissioner to Ashanti. (This is an extraordinarily compact, neat looking fort which could serve as a prototype for model forts!)

It was only a decade since King Prempeh, the Asantehene and his close relatives had been exiled to the Seychelles in a rather cynical act of 'protection' by the British authorities. The explanation for such devious dealings was that, apart from local tribal feuds, the French and Germans had designs on Ashanti and that Prempeh was a potential mischief-maker. However that did not really excuse such ruthless high-handedness. It is fascinating that it was not until Guggisberg was Governor that Prempeh was allowed home!

On the other hand there had been a sinister, fetish-related side to Kumasi, which means place of death. For ritual human sacrifices were carried out, especially on the death of a chief (apparently to provide servants for him in the next life), but also for other inexcusable reasons. Yet there was and still is a great tradition of hospitality to strangers in Ashanti, as the Guggisbergs found in their journey through the bush.

On sober reflection, however, one must admit that the repeated, ritual killings in Kumasi were not really any more culpable and often less numerous than the repeated, ritual killings of the innocent, often by nominal Christians, in terrorism, road carnage, civil wars and two World Wars. Courageous action by Guggisberg prevented at least some of the slaughter at the Battle of Loos in 1915; we will study that soon.

One interesting episode witnessed at Kumasi was the third (and final) day of a palaver held by the Chief Commissioner

Kumasi Fort. It seems almost incredible that this small fort
withstood a siege of three months in 1900, with the Governor,
Sir Frederick Hodgson and Lady Hodgson among those trapped.
Only a few years later the Guggisbergs stayed there as guests of the
Chief Commissioner for Ashanti, Mr (later Sir) Francis Fuller.

to resolve a dispute between three tribal groups. He had
already listened, in the square outside the fort, for two hot
days, eight hours a day, to long harangues on the case. After
giving judgement he disappeared into the fort and what
followed seems to have resembled the verbal abuse and
minor skirmishing one associates with the end of a football
match, when the supporters disagree with the referee! Stones
were thrown, but thanks to the intervention of one brave
African policeman (quite a small man physically) no serious
injury was done and all three groups went their separate
ways.

After dinner that evening the Guggisbergs gave what may

The Kwahu Escarpment. Photographed at the edge of a heavy thunderstorm in March 1972. The Guggisbergs' travels in the bush took them through such rough territory.

have been the first theatrical performance in Kumasi and Decima and Mr Fuller entertained the guests, the entire European community of just over twenty people, to three hours of singing.

Their progress, generally south-eastwards towards Accra, took them through dense forest, interspersed with highly fertile clearings, where intensive cultivation of cocoa trees and oil-palms was developing – a hot, well-watered area of great potential, just waiting for the rail and road developments which would eventually be constructed during Guggisberg's governorship. As a surveyor he was mapping the country. What dreams and plans for the future were even then in his mind and shared with his ambitious wife?

As 'FGG' warned in his Preface, their progress and, even

more, its description becomes a complicated 'ramble': palavers with chiefs, comments on social customs and the daily problems of achieving a remarkably civilized lifestyle despite primitive surroundings; but there were several fascinating, though simple, tales of their unique experiences, of which the following is a good example worthy of more detailed description.

Chapter XI

'A BUSH CAMP'
(WITH SUPERB STANDARDS
OF SERVICE!)

'A Bush Camp' is the title of Chapter XVI of *We Two in West Africa*. It and some other related narrative make a fascinating vignette among the massive details of the Guggisbergs' travels.

'We were up at 5.30 and before six were tackling a good solid English breakfast by candle-light (porridge, bacon and eggs, toast, marmalade, butter and coffee) . . . before we had finished, beds, clothes-boxes, baths, everything except the breakfast table had been packed up.'

The early start was hampered by particularly treacherous walking surfaces, from heavy dew, steep hills and jagged rocky outcrops, so bad that Decima had to walk with the unexpected aid of an alpenstock. This Swiss souvenir had presumably been on a bearer's head until required!

Then, just before midday, they arrived at a little clearing where the path had been widened to allow 'cookie' to prepare 'tiffin'. He and an assistant, with 'chop-boxes', had gone ahead of the main party. *'Over a little fire, hot soup, tongue, fried plantains, boiled yams, tinned peas and milk pudding'* were almost ready. Within five minutes of the Guggisbergs finishing their 'snack', everything had been cleared away and they rested while their staff adjourned to a nearby village for their own well-earned repast. Then a crowd from the village, led by the headman, arrived with *"a dash" (present) of bananas, pineapples, yams, plantains, eggs and palm wine'* – typical of the generosity of these country folk.

The going was rough all afternoon, four hours being required for six miles. Their camp for the night was to be by the Anum River which was forded easily enough as it was the middle of the dry season (it was about eighty feet across and three feet deep). They saw the dugout canoe which would have been needed to cross in the wet season and, even with that boat, the passage would have been very long and difficult, as during the rains there were miles of swamp and floodwater on both sides of the swollen river.

The going had been so bad that afternoon that many of the carriers were late. A clearing had been prepared, but there was no sign of the Guggisbergs' green tent. The reason was that one of the porters, a tough and usually reliable Hausa was very slow and had to be helped with his burden by one of the temporarily redundant hammock-boys. In fact the Hausa had almost lost a toe on the rough track.

As night fell the cook was busy preparing dinner, another man tended the lamps, yet another heated Decima's bathwater and her husband, with the aid of the medicine chest, dressed the wounded foot of the Hausa. Guggisberg, even then, had the makings of a 'Servant King'.

This conscientious caring for their staff is also well illustrated by the following comment. *'Before dinner we went to see our carriers' camp ... We found our men in a small farm*

42

Illustration from *We Two in West Africa*, 1909. The Guggisberg's camp by the Anum River (permission of William Heinemann.)

clearing containing one hut and a plantation of plantains ... In spite of their seventeen mile march along the awful road the carriers were all cheerful and contented.'

The Guggisbergs did not quite go to the extreme of dining in formal evening dress, as some British did in the bush, but they did change after bathing, Decima into a white skirt and cool blouse, Gordon into a light tropical khaki uniform. Both wore knee-length soft buckskin boots for protection – *'the Coast mosquito's happiest hunting ground is the human ankle'* (an observation still relevant!).

We Two became almost poetic as they contemplated their

awesome surroundings: the vast forest; the huge trunks of the high timber; the myriads of stars reflected in the river. Under the protection of their mosquito nets, their drift into sleep was occasionally interrupted by sounds from the wilderness, including the hoarse 'cough' of a leopard.

Much of this unique journey – for example the last stage through the Aburi Hills and Aburi Botanic Gardens to Accra – has not been detailed here, but hopefully the reader should by now have some inkling of how the Guggisbergs and the many Africans who worked for them or whom they met gradually developed a mutual understanding and friendship which boded well for their future relationships.

To round off discussion of this book a few points are worth mention: first, that more often it conveys a message from her, sometimes from him, sometimes less specific and presumably from both; second, despite the obviously efficient organizing of their expeditions, one also senses a relaxed and happy atmosphere; yet occasionally a more imperial note is sounded. The last point will be discussed later, when we consider the broader aspects of the nature of the unique leadership of Gordon Guggisberg and his place in colonial history.

Chapter XII

HANDBOOK OF THE SOUTHERN NIGERIA SURVEY AND TEXTBOOK OF TOPOGRAPHICAL SURVEYING IN TROPICAL AFRICA (1911)

This is a detailed, but disciplined report, quite different from the chatty nature of *We Two*. It reflects Guggisberg's ability, not just as a professional surveyor, but also as a meticulous organizer and enthusiastic teacher. A succinct appreciation of this publication by Sir Charles Close, the Director-General of the Ordnance Survey, appears in Lord Olivier's biography:

> The duties of all members of the staff were strictly defined and, in particular, sensible rules were laid down as to the relations of the staff with the civil administration. Much attention was paid to the treatment of villagers; unpaid labour was forbidden; all goods bought were to be paid for at the recognised rate; and great care was to be exercised not to damage the crops ... They were model instructions and the survey of Nigeria was a model survey.

It is not surprising that Guggisberg wrote with authority on surveying in Africa, for he spent about a fifth of his life in

that occupation – from 1902 to 1914. His appointments were
as follows:

1902 Assistant Director, Special Survey of Gold Coast and
Ashanti; 1905, promoted Director of Survey of Gold Coast
and Ashanti: 1908 posted to Chatham for regimental duties
(*We Two* was written at that time); 1910, Director of Southern
Nigeria Survey (1911, published report on this); 1913, (after
union of Southern and Northern Nigeria) became Director of
Nigeria Survey. (Wraith discusses in detail the battle that
Guggisberg had with Sir Frederick Lugard, Governor of
Nigeria, to get the eventual promotion.)

The *Handbook* starts with a clear, concise description of the
geography of Southern Nigeria (he was already a Fellow of
the Royal Geographical Society). The aims of the survey
were generally to build on that broader knowledge and were
four-fold: topographical, cadastral, educational and
meteorological. Again we see the amazing overview that
Guggisberg had of West Africa, functional as well as
structural. A realist as well as a dreamer he pointed out how
map-making had to keep within the limits of a budget – *'a
fair mean should be struck between the conflicting demands of
accuracy and economy.'*
He also insisted that detailed maps should initially be
drawn in the field, within the broader zones of the standard
maps of the country. Even an amateur can appreciate the
difficulties of accurate surveying in that territory, much of it
hilly, intersected by numerous meandering rivers and partly
impassable in forest areas.
The precise staffing, European and African, was spelt out.

A survey school was established for the training of surveyors (topographical and cadastral), meteorologists and draughtsmen. Nobody in the survey was left in any doubt as to his duties and position in the chain of command. Guggisberg was well-intentioned, enlightened and progressive, but would brook no sloth, incompetence or shady dealing. Thus, in para 22 of the report:

> *Warning to Surveyors on Promotion. All survey officials are warned that should they on promotion to a higher grade, slacken their energies and diminish their out-turn, their grade will be promptly reduced. Annual increments will not be recommended unless the surveyor's work is entirely satisfactory.*
>
> [In para 24] *Presents. Gratuities and Payments. Any member of the Southern Nigeria Survey who can be proved to have received, on any pretence whatsoever, any present or gratuity from his subordinates or from the inhabitants of districts in which he may have been or is employed, will be summarily dismissed.*

What was described as *'unfaithful work'* – either careless or intentional would also be punished.

Rules about payment to workers who were off work from sickness or injury were also strict. Broadly, they were given full pay if they had not personally contributed to the illness or injury; if culpable, they were not paid. *'Any man developing gonorrhoea or a similar complaint will be at once discharged.'*

Guggisberg was becoming so involved in Africa that he contemplated leaving the Army. In fact in 1914 he was in the process of being appointed as Director of Public Works for the Gold Coast, when the First World War intervened and, in anticipation of this, he sailed for Britain.

When he returned to the Gold Coast in 1919, Major Guggisberg had become Brigadier-General Guggisberg and the man in command. When that did occur his top priority was to promote the universal education of the Africans. He had been so impressed with their intellectual potential in survey work and other contacts with them, that he was determined their potential should be realized.

Chapter XIII

GUGGISBERG IN THE
FIRST WORLD WAR

Major Guggisberg knew nothing of the start of the War –
he was unconscious in a London nursing home; at the
time of the Armistice Brigadier-General Guggisberg was one
of three Deputy Inspector Generals responsible for training
on the Western Front. His war service, like so much of his
life, was more amazing than fiction.

One morning in July 1914, when war threatened, but was
not yet inevitable, Guggisberg was on his way to Lords,
having just decided to resign his Army Commission and
accept the post of Director of Public Works in the Gold
Coast. In fact he had letters about these two decisions in his
pocket as he rounded the Marble Arch on his way to an
afternoon's cricket. But he lost control of his unstable bicycle
(apparently a kind of prehistoric moped) and crashed,
fracturing the base of his skull. As he lay in a nursing home,
the War started without him!

His return to consciousness was slow, but, as soon as he
understood the situation, he became a very difficult patient
and forced his discharge, long before he was really fit. He
destroyed the letters relating to his proposed change of status
and the Colonial Office and War Office confirmed that he
was still in the Regular Army.

However it was three months before he was passed medically fit for home service, five months for overseas service and finally a year before he went to the Western Front. His first posting was as Officer Commanding the 94th Field Company of the Royal Engineers, a small unit of Kitchener's volunteer army; he found the training of two hundred civilians from scratch to cope with the basics of military engineering a task to his liking.

Across the Channel it was another world. The horrors of trench warfare were such that even he could never have imagined it – men maimed and massacred in their thousands for a few yards of mud. However it is not intended here to enter into futile attempts to explain the madness of those tragic days. Let us concentrate on how the War affected Guggisberg and what influence he had on its battles.

His unit was in the 19th Division and took part in the Battle of Loos in September 1915. Thousands of men had been mowed down by machine-gun fire on barbed wire guarding the German trenches. Another attack was to be made, despite the apparent failure of the artillery to destroy the barbed-wire entanglements. Then Guggisberg personally surveyed the wire opposite his own brigade, an act of great courage in the face of enemy fire, and reported to his Brigadier that the wire *was* intact and that a further attack would be suicidal. At first his advice was ignored, but he continued his protestations and eventually their urgency persuaded the Brigadier to cancel the attack. (Wraith quotes a letter by a Colonel R.F.A. Butterworth in which he stated: 'I am positive that his brave and independent action saved his Brigade from an appalling disaster.')

Guggisberg's courage and capability had been proved in a crisis, but he also showed outstanding tenacity in coping with the never-ending work of the Royal Engineers in repairing the repeated destruction of defences by enemy artillery and mortars. In this he drove his men hard, himself even harder, despite never being really fit, from trouble with his legs and recurrent malaria. His qualities soon led to his promotion to Lieutenant Colonel and Commander, Royal Engineers (CRE) of the 8th Division, a regular formation.

The 8th Division for a time enjoyed a period of comparative calm before the holocaust of the Somme. Characteristically, Guggisberg used the time to devise '*an RE Programme of Work to assist the Infantry in a Brigade Sector*'. (This received commendation in the *History of the Corps of Royal Engineers.*)

During the battle of the Somme Guggisberg, exhausted by his unsparing efforts, became seriously ill with pneumonia and yet another recurrence of malaria and was given two months' sick leave in England (September and October 1916).

On recovery he was appointed CRE of the 66th (2nd East Lancashire) Division. His ability as an instructor is recorded in the *History of the East Lancashire Royal Engineers* – thus 'on arrival in France the field companies got their first chance to practise the long, detailed, but well thought out maxims of the CRE, Lt. Col. F.G. Guggisberg.' Yet again he showed his uncanny capacity for clarifying a complicated situation.

He next received what for an engineer officer was a rare honour – promotion to Brigadier-General in command of an infantry brigade (the 170th). On appointment, he attended a training school for senior officers and this had an extra bonus, because on that course there started his friendship with Lieutenant Colonel J.H. Levey, who was commandant of the course and also had experience of West Africa. Sadly his brigade was soon to suffer severe casualties in the battle of Passchendaele.

Fortunately Guggisberg survived and for the last six months of the War was given work for which he was ideally suited, in a new training establishment which was urgently needed because so many of the troops were recently recruited and dangerously inexperienced. The Inspector General in command was Lieutenant General Sir Ivor Maxse and his chief staff officer was Colonel Levey, who lost no time in proposing his friend Guggisberg as one of the three Deputy Inspector Generals to be appointed. Maxse agreed, as he already had first-hand experience of Guggisberg's ability as a training officer. Needless to say, Guggisberg was an outstanding success in this rôle even as Wraith records, using his enthusiasm for cricket to invent games for machine-gun practice – what he called 'net practice'!

Such courageous and skilful war service did not go unnoted and Guggisberg was five times mentioned in despatches, was awarded the Distinguished Service Order and became a Chevalier of the Legion of Honour. Yet his heart was in Africa and, sooner than he might have hoped, it was there his greatest honour was to come. His appointment under Sir Ivor Maxse may have been a factor in his becoming Governor of the Gold Coast, for Maxse was soon to be Lord Milner's brother-in-law, and it was Lord Milner, as

Colonial Secretary, who chose Guggisberg for that high office. Let us, however, pause a little before looking at the complex lobbying which preceded that decision.

Chapter XIV

MRS GUGGISBERG'S WAR

Decima made a magnificent war effort, which was recognized with the CBE and the *Médaille de Reconnaissance Française, Première Classe*. Her work was first with the Women's Emergency Corps; then she organized a leave club in Paris for serving British officers, a similar club for the French Army and, at the end of the War, the British Empire Leave Club in Cologne, whither she had followed her husband. Her vivacity, enthusiasm and energy were ideally suited to this type of high-class public relations work. She met and became well acquainted with many eminent people in the course of these activities and, in consequence, she herself became a lady of considerable importance.

In fact, by the end of the War, both the Guggisbergs had, independently of each other, attained a status which would not easily be satisfied by any ordinary position, such as that of a technical officer and his wife. Decima decided that no stone should be left unturned to further Gordon's career.

Chapter XV

DISAPPOINTMENT: THEN APPOINTMENT!

Late in the War, Guggisberg applied to be considered for the post of Chief Commissioner for the Northern Territory of the Gold Coast, an area which he considered to have great potential. He was turned down, mainly because of Governor Sir Hugh Clifford's opposition, with the rather weak excuse that he (Guggisberg) 'lacked administrative experience'. (The higher echelons of the colonial administration were a jealously guarded closed shop, seldom breached by outsiders even of outstanding qualities – surely a handicap to optimal efficiency and development.)

Thus far, then, Director of Public Works seemed the only career open in the Gold Coast. But Guggisberg would have been frustrated in a largely technical post, a rôle of secondary status, and the high-flying Decima would never have tolerated anything but the top of the colony's social scale. So both, especially Decima, cast around among friends and other contacts for support in furthering an administrative career in Africa.

Guggisberg could expect no help from the establishment of the colonial service despite his outstanding record as a surveyor. Although he had made a great success of his military duties in the War, help from contemporaries and even superiors in rank could only be of marginal importance in helping to re-establish his career in West Africa. Those who served under him in the Royal Engineers would almost certainly have backed him for high office, but, sadly, such potentially important referees are seldom consulted.

It is fascinating that even today, when one is discussing the life of Sir Gordon Guggisberg with friends (I hope they remain so!), one gets a message from the past that there was a kind of club, membership of which had been service under Guggisberg either in the Royal Engineers or The Gold Coast.

Wraith discusses information from several sources about the backing Guggisberg had from various people. Most of the running was made by Decima and her lobbying was eventually aimed at Lord Milner who had recently become Secretary of State for the Colonies. She had apparently met Lord Milner at her leave club in Paris, when he visited it as a member of the War Cabinet, but probably didn't know him very well. Her main influence on him was exerted indirectly through Elinor Glyn the novelist, with whom she had a much closer relationship. Elinor Glyn was a war correspondent in Paris, was involved with Decima's Club and was a close friend of Lord Milner. Gossip suggested a scandalous element to the 'wire-pulling' but this was denied, and indeed, Guggisberg had a special meeting with Elinor Glyn before she would even put forward his case to Lord Milner for appointment to a senior administrative post, and specifically to the Governorship of the Gold Coast. Guggisberg was then invited to visit Lord Milner, who was very favourably impressed with his personality, his highly successful career and the short- and long-term plans he suggested for that part of Africa, which he obviously knew so well. As already mentioned, Sir Ivor Maxse may also have influenced the decision. Yet, the more one learns of the high ideals of Viscount Milner, his recognition that imperial unity should be balanced by the proper recognition of the uniqueness and aspirations of the component nations of the Empire and his untiring capacity for hard and detailed work, the more one senses that in Guggisberg he found someone who shared his idealism particularly in relation to education and had proved his ability to get things done. And there may well have been another, hidden element in Milner's decision – namely a German one. Milner's paternal grandmother was German; he spent much of his early life in Germany, even being partly educated at a gymnasium in Tübingen and spending a holiday with his father walking behind the German lines in the Franco-Prussian War! He admired German hard work and organization and was accused by his detractors in Britain as being more German than British. Thus the German-Swiss element in Guggisberg may also have influenced his decision. The tacit assumption that, although Guggisberg's Governorship was a success, his appointment was made for the wrong reasons appears to be insulting to Lord Milner's intelligence, integrity and what has been called his 'mellow sanity'.

The vacancy for the Governorship of the Gold Coast was due to Sir Hugh Clifford's appointment as Governor of Nigeria. Clifford never really recovered from learning that he was to be succeeded by Guggisberg! It was only a short time since he had turned down Guggisberg for the post of Chief Commissioner for the Northern Territory, what was considered the least important part of the Colony. Clifford, who regarded Guggisberg as a 'mountebank', criticized him at every opportunity. It is not the intention in this short biography to go into the complexities of their relationship (that hopefully will be done in another publication), but Clifford may well have felt frustrated that *his* plans for development were put in cold storage because of the War, which lasted for most of his rule, whereas *Guggisberg* was given the green light for his schemes.

However, there is one story of their relationship, detailed by Wraith, but well worth retelling. When about to return to the Gold Coast from leave, Guggisberg noticed that Clifford was booked for Nigeria on the same ship as himself from Liverpool. He arranged to have his booking transferred to the next ship, sailing two weeks later. Clifford, also, had seen the initial passenger list, and he, too, transferred to the next ship. Whether by accident, mischievous design or fear of these formidable gentlemen, nobody in the shipping agent's staff pointed out the situation, and they embarked together at Liverpool. Apparently they avoided each other like the plague during the whole voyage – amusing, yet sad!

The more personal aspects of their antipathy may never be explained, but their paths to high office were so disparate that they had little of common experience on which to come to a working relationship. Indeed the first fifty years of Guggisberg's life provided a truly unique sequence of experiences. It is to his eternal credit that he moulded these by his enthusiasm, courage, humanity, hard work and natural ability into an enlightening course in self-education which ensured the success of his greatest venture.

Chapter XVI

GOVERNOR GUGGISBERG
OPENS HIS INNINGS

There was no tentative playing in. He struck with the power of a West African tornado. His dreams and schemes had been maturing over many years. He was ready for action. He knew the country; he knew its peoples; he recognized the tremendous potentials of both; and he had decided views on what was needed to fulfil them.

Most importantly, education must be made universally available for the ordinary African. But, to pay for this, trade must be expanded, which, in turn, depended on improvements in transport – a deepwater harbour with associated rail and road developments. Health care must also be enhanced, otherwise the people would not be able to cope with sustained hard work or intensive education.

In this biography detailed documentation has been kept as brief as is compatible with conveying understanding. However, some of the correspondence, despatches and associated comments at this critical time in Guggisberg's Governorship are so vital that they should be seen in their original form.

On 12 August 1919, Guggisberg wrote to Lord Milner accepting the Governorship. The accompanying photocopy of this letter is shown as it was his first item of correspondence to Lord Milner after the appointment and in which he was also to refer to the relatively modest allowance of £300 for the expenses he would incur in taking up residence in the Gold Coast.

29, Half Moon Street,
Piccadilly, W.
R.C° 12 August, 1919.
Rec¹ 14 AUG 19

Your Lordship,

I have the honour to acknowledge the receipt of your Lordship's letter informing me that H.M. The King, has been pleased to approve of my appointment as Governor and Commander-in-Chief of the Gold Coast.

If your Lordship approves, I suggest that the 17th September will be a suitable date for embarcation.

Referring to the last paragraph of your Lordship's letter, I should be glad if the £300 mentioned could be paid to my bankers, Messrs. Cox & Co., 16 Charing Cross, S.W.

I have the honour to be,

Your Lordship's most obedient

humble Servant

[signature]
Brig. General.

The Right Hon.
Viscount Milner, G.C.B., G.C.M.G.,
The Colonial Office,
Downing Street, S.W.

He sailed for the 'Coast" on 24 September, a week later than suggested in the letter. The intervening six weeks were packed with the intensive study of the situation he would face and frenetic contacting of individuals who might help his cause. His preparations were so advanced that, even before he left England, he was able, on 19 September, to send a detailed 'Preliminary Report on Transportation in the Gold Coast Colony' with a covering letter to Lord Milner, asking for permission to start work on various items and to raise loans for the ventures. A considerable part of the 'Report' now follows to show the magnitude and complexity of the task that Guggisberg had undertaken and his grasp of how it should be accomplished.

London.
September 19th. 1919.

A PRELIMINARY REPORT ON TRANSPORTATION IN THE GOLD COAST COLONY

1.   *A definite transportation policy is necessary for the development of the immensely valuable resources in Agriculture, Minerals and Forestry of the Gold Coast Colony for the following reasons:-*

Trade in   *(a) Under existing conditions the present productivity*
the South   *of the country from the sea up to and including the Southern portions of Ashanti is greatly in excess of available means of mechanical transport. In the absence, owing to the Tsetse fly, of any possibility of animal draught by far the greater part of transport is on the heads of natives. This is not only so expensive*

62

as to prevent the paying development of industries such as the Oil Palm and certain inland mineral deposits, but is wasteful of the man power necessary for the agricultural development of the country. This wastage, in view of the comparatively thin population, is particularly serious.

Owing to the lack of mechanical transport, the trade of what may be called the more fully developed portions of the country is not a quarter of what it should be. When it is considered that an efficient transport will more than pay for itself it is at once apparent that any neglect on our part to provide this transport means that we are deliberately throwing money away, an action which would not be tolerated for one moment by the shareholders in any commercial undertaking. The only further comment that appears necessary is that the natives of the country are the principal shareholders in this matter of trade.[1]

Trade in the North

(b) Serious as is the transportation question in the (at present) more productive parts of the country, it is still graver when we consider the great tracts of country (over half the total area) which lie to the North of Coomassie.[2] In the Northern Territories and the Northern parts of Ashanti the present production of Ground Nuts and Shea Butter is such as to foreshadow really enormous expansion of a trade of great value. Both present production and future development are so severely handicapped by lack of transport as to render paying trade prohibitive.

1. This sentence gives a vital clue to his commitment to the advancement of the African.
2. This spelling, Coomassie, was commonly used at that time; now usually Kumasi.

63

Cattle Trade (c) *Further, the Northern Territories is natural ground for the establishment of a great cattle industry. The value of this to the remainder of the Colony is very great in view of the existence of what might almost be called 'a meat famine'. Owing to the action of neighbouring powers in diverting their cattle routes for their own purpose the situation daily becomes more serious. Such an industry would further develop into a trade of hides and fat and possibly of frozen meat with the United Kingdom. But any question of establishing a cattle industry is absolutely dependent on the existence of railway communication with the Northern Territories.*

General increase in Trade (d) *I have lately had interview with the Canadian Trade Mission, with the result that both Mr. Lloyd Harris (the head of the Mission) and I are convinced that we can open a large mutual trade direct between the Gold Coast and Canada. I am shortly interviewing the South African Trade Mission on a similar subject as I foresee a large import of South African wines in view of the probable future prohibition of gin or of very high import duties on the latter.[3]*

Result of not providing transport (e) *Summing up, it is clear that if we do not provide proper transport we shall be responsible for:*
(I) Deliberately handicapping the development of trade in the Southern portion of the whole country to the financial loss alike of the native producer, the merchant and the Government, and to the wastage of

---

3. The importing of rum from Cuba was also in process of being prohibited – an additional blow to the economy because of loss of import duty.

man power urgently needed for agricultural and other purposes.

(II) Deliberately retarding to such an extent as to stop almost entirely the trade development of a country which is potentially rich in agricultural and cattle breeding possibilities i.e. the Northern Territories.

(III) Handicapping to such an extent as to lose daily a large proportion of trade with the United Kingdom and the Colonies and Dominions of the Empire, a trade which it should be our duty to foster to the utmost possible extent.

Urgency of a Transporta-tion Policy (f) Finally a settlement of a clearly defined policy is not only necessary to prevent waste of railway and Public Works, it is urgent owing to the time that will be taken in constructing roads and railways and to the fact that the war, while not retarding the growth of agriculture, has seriously affected transport developments.

2.   *THE TRANSPORTATION PROBLEM[4]*
The Transportation problem of the Gold Coast Colony comprises:-
(a) A deep-sea harbour.
(b) Railways converging on this harbour at such a distance apart as will render them accessible by light motor transport from all parts of the country.
(c) Main motor roads for light lorry transport to railways.
(d) Minor roads for feeding the main motor roads either by light motor tractors or hand drawn carts.

---

4. More precisely the suggested solution to the problem.

3. *HARBOUR*

(a) There can be no possible doubt that the Gold Coast requires one deep-sea harbour, without which any further development of the country by railway and road will be useless, as the latter will bring such increased trade that our present embarkation facilities will be unable to deal with it. The site most suitable for a deep-sea harbour is undoubtedly in the neighbourhood of Seccondee. No estimate of the cost is yet possible, but it may be taken that the harbour will cost at least £2,000,000. Even should it cost double that amount the money will be well spent, as the present system of a number of small ports on a coast line just over 300 miles in length, served by surf boats, and in a few instances by barges, leads to great losses in stores, waste of labour, and loss of time and money to traders and shipping alike. The system no doubt originated in the past from the absence of railways: its continued existence in the future is unjustifiable. The deep-sea harbour will constitute both directly and indirectly a source of revenue sufficient to meet interest and sinking fund charges – in fact it will pay for itself.

(b) The first step is the selection of the site, and the execution of a careful survey on which the cost can be estimated. The survey of the Seccondee waters should be placed in hand at once. Once the plan is settled the funds from a loan should be immediately available so that the work can be placed in hand at once and energetically carried out. Every day lost in the completion of this harbour means a definite amount of trade and revenue lost.

(c) *With regard to selection of site. I suggest that the preliminary surveys should be undertaken at the earliest possible date by Messrs. Stewart and McDonnell, and that should their estimate prove satisfactory, they should be entrusted with the construction of the harbour. Messrs. Stewart and McDonnell are Canadian engineers, whose work both in Canada and the war is well-known.*

4. <u>*RAILWAYS*</u>

The settlement of a definite policy of railway construction is an all important item in the transportation problem. Without such a policy an efficient and ultimately economical plan of road-making which must proceed concurrently with railway construction, becomes impossible.

The railway construction policy should include the following points which are dealt with in detail in paragraph 5 et seq:

<u>*General plan of railway system.*</u> *The general route of each line forming part of the whole railway system by which the country will eventually be served must be laid down as a guide to all future work on transportation facilities.*

<u>*Order of construction.*</u> *The order of urgency in the construction of the various lines must be laid down.*

<u>*Method of construction.*</u> *The question of whether the lines should be built by contract or by the Gold Coast Government must be laid down.*

<u>*Cost.*</u> *The method by which the expenditure will be met should be settled.*

5. ## GENERAL PLAN OF THE RAILWAY SYSTEM

The main railway system must be such that every part of the country will eventually be within easy reach of the various lines by light motor transport. This distance should not be greater than about 40-50 miles.

On my arrival in the Gold Coast a special 'Transportation Committee' will be formed of those Government officers, merchants and natives whose knowledge of the country and various local experiences will give weight to their opinion. It is hoped by the end of November a map showing the most useful distribution of railways will be available.

[He really was in a hurry!]

6. ## REMARKS ON THE PROPOSED RAILWAY SYSTEM

(I) THE GREAT NORTHERN RAILWAY

(a) Approximate route. Seccondee-Coomassie-Atabobo-Tamale-Gambaga.

(b) Approximate length. 518 miles; of this distance Seccondee to Coomassie (168 miles) is built, but about 150 miles will require wholesale reconstruction. The total length of new construction will therefore be 500 miles.

(c) Object. To develop trade in Northern Ashanti and the Northern Territories, including the Northern portion of Togoland coming under our mandate.

(II) SOUTH EASTERN RAILWAY

(a) Route. As at present located i.e. Accra-Tafo-Kwahu-Coomassie.

(b) Length. 200 miles, of which 72 miles from Accra

68

to *Tafo have been constructed and the remainder pegged out. Construction required is 128 miles, of which 22 miles have already been cleared and earth works completed.*

(c) Object. Has been fully dealt with in the Acting Governor's despatch of 15th July 1919 (C.O. 45432).[5] I fully concur in the necessity for the immediate completion of this railway.

(III) WESTERN FRONTIER RAILWAY
(a) Approximate route. From a point on the Great Northern railway between Seccondee and Dunkwa to Wa.

(IV) SECCONDEE KWAHU RAILWAY
(a) Approximate route. Seccondee-Manso-Nsawam-Kwahu. [Guggisberg doubted the value of this route which had been discussed by Slater and thought the Transportation Committee should review it.]

7.   *USES OF TOPOGRAPHICAL SURVEY IN RAILWAY LOCATION*
Without entering into technical details it is desirable to determine the most economical manner in which a railway, after its general route has been settled, should be exactly located on the ground.
[Guggisberg then emphasised (at length) the importance of proper surveys in the light of his

---

5. This document, from the Acting Governor, Mr A.R. Slater, was as long and detailed as Guggisberg's 'Preliminary Report'. It was set aside at the Colonial Office with the brief, handwritten comment, 'Reply to await appointment of new Governor'. It may have been initiated by Mr A.R. Slater as part of a bid for permanent promotion, but Sir Hugh Clifford may have been behind it, as a Parthian shot to pre-empt Guggisberg's expected onslaught.

Nigerian experiences and how they could help
choose the optimum route and save money.]

8. ORDER OF URGENCY IN
    CONSTRUCTION
    In arranging the order of construction the principle
    should be observed that as many lines as labour will
    permit should be under construction at one time to
    make up for the loss of time caused by the war and to
    bring nearer the date on which it may be possible to
    place all parts of the country within reasonable reach
    of the railway.
    Item 1. THE RECONSTRUCTION OF THE
    GREATER PART OF THE SECCONDEE-
    COOMASSIE LINE is of first importance [as
    emphasised by the Acting Governor].
        The Line is now in such bad condition as to be
    unable to cope with the traffic; it is extravagant in
    running owing to its continual curves and bad
    grading, and there is reason to believe that the bridges
    will not long stand the work expected of them. It is no
    exaggeration to say that at any moment we may have
    a serious breakdown in the system. Approval for the
    whole scheme of reconstruction is urgently required
    and I would ask that authority for the survey and
    pegging out to start forthwith should be cabled to the
    Acting Governor.
    Item 2. Concurrently with Item 1, the COM-
    PLETION OF THE TAFO-COOMASSIE
    LINE should be taken in hand at once.
    Item 3. The PRELIMINARY TOPO-
    GRAPHICAL SURVEYS FOR THE
    EXTENSION OF THE GREAT NORTHERN

70

RAILWAY from COOMASSIE-GAMBAGA, AND THE WESTERN FRONTIER AND SECCONDEE-KWAHU RAILWAYS should proceed concurrently with the work mentioned in Items 1 and 2, as they can be executed by the Survey Department. I propose to issue instructions for this work as soon as the Transportation Committee has settled the best general routes.

Item 4. When the work of Item 3 has advanced sufficiently the EXACT LOCATION OF THE COOMASSIE/GAMBAGA SECTION should be undertaken by the railway engineers, the line pegged out and estimates prepared for approval.

Item 5. The CONSTRUCTION OF THE COOMASSIE GAMBAGA RAILWAY should begin immediately that labour is available. I feel reasonably sure, and in this Capt. Armitage agrees with me, that when the Northern Territory Chiefs know that the extension of the railway to their country can be begun when labour is available, they will find the necessary men without depleting the mines of the labour required. Without being unduly optimistic I foresee the possibility of beginning the construction of this very important line before work on Items 1 and 2 is complete.

Item 6. The LOCATION AND CONSTRUC-TION OF THE WESTERN FRONTIER AND THE SECONDEE KWAHU lines will probably have to wait until the survey parties on Items 1 and 4, and the labour parties on Items 1 and 2, are free.

9.   *METHOD OF RAILWAY CONSTRUCTION*
(a) I am strongly in favour of the Government

71

Railway Department building all the new railways. The very fact that the Department is building railways for its own use will tend to give it such an interest in the work as will be productive of efficiency and economy. I am a firm believer in esprit de corps *being the secret of success in any department: This spirit is usually well marked in Railway Departments and should be fostered to the utmost. To call in outside contractors would not foster the spirit, besides leading to probable friction.*

(b) To construct our own railways we shall have to form a large construction branch of the present Railway Department. I am not prepared at the moment to submit exact details of organisation, but generally I think we should form the staff entirely of men who will come on the permanent and pensionable employment list of the Colony. There is ample railway work for many years to come, and as construction work gradually decreases the construction staff can be gradually utilised to fill vacancies in other branches of the Railway, the Public Works Department, etc.

(c) The pay of the Construction Staff should be met out of the loan.

10. ### COST OF RAILWAYS

The cost of the new lines will amount approximately to £14,000,000, of which about £4,000,000 will be required during the next four years. This amount is made up as follows:-

1. Seccondee-Coomassie Railway	£1,000,000
2. Tafo-Coomassie Railway	1,670,000
3. Location of the Coomassie-Gambaga Railway	40,000
4. Construction of the first 100 miles of the Coomassie-Gambaga Railway	1,300,000
Total	£4,010,000

In his despatch of the 15th July 1919 (C.O. 45432) The Acting Governor asks for a loan of £3,000,000 to cover the cost of certain items mentioned in paragraph 21 of the despatch referred to. I think that this amount should be altered to read £4,000,000 and that the loan should be for the purpose of Railway construction only.

11.

MOTOR ROADS

Until the Transportation Committee has decided on the general plan of the railway system little purpose would be served by going into details of the motor roads required for feeding the railways.

I consider however that £125,000 per annum is the least that we should expend for the next four years on these motor roads. This money cannot fairly for the present be found out of revenue which will be severely enough taxed in finding the amount necessary for upkeep. I propose, with his Lordship's approval, to raise the £500,000 required for the next four years by the issue of Government Bonds in the Gold Coast and Ashanti.

F.G. Guggisberg
GOVERNOR

The 'Preliminary Report' was accompanied by the following letter to Lord Milner:

London
19th September 1919

My Lord,
  1. I have the honour to submit for your Lordship's consideration the attached 'Preliminary Report on Transportation in the Gold Coast Colony'.
  2. Although it would appear somewhat early in my Governorship to submit a report of this nature, my knowledge of the country and my study of despatches of the last few month justifies me in giving general proposals. They are of such a nature that they are applicable to any colony situated as is the Gold Coast. Further experience will only necessitate alteration in details, and these, as I have pointed out in Para 5 of the Report, will be forthcoming in due course from the Transportation Committee.
  3. I would ask for Your Lordship's approval now of the following points in the Report:-
  (1) General approval of the adoption of the definite policy given in para 2 of the Report.
  (2) Approval for the engagement of the services of the firm mentioned in para 3 (c) of the Report for survey of the harbour site.
  (3) Approval for the expenses of this harbour survey being met by the Gold Coast Government out of revenue, repayable from the loan that will be required for the harbour when such is floated.
  (4) Approval of the order of urgency in Railway Construction as given in para 8 of the Report.
  (5) Approval of the system of construction as given in para 9 of the Report.
  (6) Approval for a loan of £4,000, 000 for the purpose given in para 10.

(7) Approval for the principle of the proposal in para 11, details of the suggested method of issue of the bonds to be forwarded later for Your Lordship's approval.

4. In conclusion, I have on several occasions lately pointed out to Mercantile and Mining Firms, and to the London Chamber of Commerce, that such charges as railway rates and cocoa taxes can only be reduced if efficient transportation facilities exist. The success of a loan for transportation services in the Gold Coast is, I understand, assured provided that it is floated before the Spring.
I have the honour to be,
Your Lordship's humble obedient servant,

Governor.

The Right Honourable
Viscount Milner, G.C.B.

One must applaud Guggisberg's principles and admire his enthusiasm, but it all leaves one a little breathless. He had hit a straight six out of the ground in the first over! The 'Preliminary Report' certainly shook the Colonial Office, where there was a particularly strident response from Mr W.D. Ellis, one of the senior civil servants. He commented thus:

I am rather sorry that General Guggisberg did not wait until he had arrived in the colony, and there considered the problem nearer at hand and at greater leisure before putting forward his very ambitious scheme for the development of transport in the Gold Coast. In [despatch] 45432 [of 15th July], Mr Slater, The Acting Governor, put forward a scheme which, in my opinion, goes to the limit of what is prudent in

75

the way of immediate expenditure. These proposals of General Guggisberg, in my opinion, go far beyond that limit, and are tainted with the disease of reckless extravagance, so prevalent among the officers who have been entrusted with the expenditure of large sums in connection with the war. The way in which officers have expended public money on development in this way is justly condemned by Sir George Buchanan[6] in his recent articles in *The Times* on Mesopotamia.

Mr Ellis did, in fact, offer some useful positive advice on the implications of the 'ambitious' plans and these were taken up by Lord Milner. We shall refer to them shortly.

The cautious and conscientious Mr Ellis reacted in an unexpectedly outraged tone, but his attitude to General Guggisberg may have been conditioned by a confidential letter he sent to Ellis on 30 August:

Confidential

29, Half Moon Street,
Piccadilly,
W1.
30th August 1919

My dear Ellis,
    Thank you for the books about the N.T. I will return them in due course.
    I thoroughly agree with you about Armitage. He is a splendid fellow and has done invaluable work for 25 years in West Africa. I sincerely hope that these services will be recognised by giving him a Governorship of the Gambia or some similar position.

---

6. A consultant civil engineer who was in charge of the reconstruction of Basra Harbour.

As you know I am going to develop the Northern Territories at once. You will agree that we want there a real live man. Also as Fuller is retiring we shall want a live man in Ashanti. To my mind Harper is the first choice and I earnestly recommend that he should be given one of these two billets. The question is which is more important of the two. Ashanti seems to be going well and the work done by Fuller will be an admirable foundation for his successor. Undoubtedly at the moment it is the more important of the two.

I do not want Harper to go too far away as he has such an invaluable knowledge of the Gold Coast. There are also one or two Chiefs in Ashanti who want firm and tactful treatment. I therefore think that Harper should now be appointed to replace Fuller and that we should obtain from Nigeria one of the second class residents from the Northern Provinces. Although not the same conditions in the Northern Provinces and the Northern Territories, they are more alike than any other of our West-African Colonies. The man I should like to have would be [name deleted from the original] *if he could be spared* [obviously he couldn't]. *If this exchange between the Gold Coast and Nigeria is not considered advisable I should like the matter to wait over until I have made the personal acquaintance of some of the Provincial Commissioners in the Gold Coast.*

I am sending in an official application for the appointment of Mr C W Pettit to be General Manager of the Gold Coast railways. I am very anxious that this appointment should be made as Pettit knows the Gold Coast well and is in my opinion fit for the job. We shall have very extensive work in Railway construction in the next ten years and it is advisable that the General Manager should, in addition to other qualities, be an Engineer.

As you know, Lord Milner wants me to make a short tour and return with my policy to see him in the Spring. As this policy will include extensive developments both in Railways, Roads and Harbour works, I am very anxious that Pettit should come out with

*me on September 24th, as there will be much work to do in
preparing estimates for work and staff.[7]*
Sincerely Yours,

W.D. Ellis Esq,
The Colonial Office,
Downing Street, S.W.

How close had Guggisberg been to Ellis before this? Possibly
not enough to justify 'My dear Ellis' which seems rather
patronizing. The flight of ideas in the letter almost gives one
the impression that with half a chance Guggisberg would
gladly have organized all the West African Colonies and
surely Clifford would not take too kindly to the transfer of
his abler Commissioners from Nigeria to the Gold Coast!
This letter may well have sensitized Ellis to the new
Governor.

The 'Preliminary Report' appears to have been circulated
among the officials of the Colonial Office and Lord Milner
wrote copious notes in his own handwriting on its
implications. Many of these were constructively critical, but
on 4 October he wrote: 'I do not share Mr Ellis's fears,
holding as I do that the Gold Coast like most of our Crown
Colonies is undercapitalised. General Guggisberg's
programme seems to me comprehensive and not
extravagant.' This note is of such importance that a
photocopy is now shown:

---

7. Within a very short time Guggisberg had managed to have Pettit appointed to the new post of
Secretary for Works with a seat on the Legislative Council!

(Crown Copyright Material in the Public Record Office.
Reproduced by kind permission of the Controller of Her Majesty's
Stationery Office. Ref. CO 96/608.21661.54356.)

Despite the criticisms by his staff and his own doubts as to
the financing of Guggisberg's transport plans, Milner did not
delay his message of qualified support, which he sent first by
telegram.

Telegram from the Secretary of State for the Colonies to the
Governor of the Gold Coast.
(Sent 3.53p.m. 13th October, 1919)

Your letter of 19th September I am inclined to approve of
your proposals in principle subject to the production of
evidence satisfactory to me and to prospective lenders that the
Colony can meet the debt charge. No Imperial guarantee can
be given. The Crown Agents have been asked to make
enquiries as to prospect of floating a loan of £4,000,000 to
£6,000,000 at an early date, and to enter into an agreement for
a report on the harbour with Stewart and McDonnell. A
despatch will follow by mail.

MILNER

The telegram was followed by a despatch giving a detailed response. Instructions by Lord Milner as to the main messages of this despatch are of particular interest and now follow:

> The telegram to the Governor should be immediately followed, as Sir G Fiddes proposes, by a despatch. I wish it to be sympathetic and to express our agreement with his general policy and our desire to support him in it. But I think it should at the same time point out the difficulties which we see and which he ought to realise. In so doing, I think good use could be made of Mr Ellis's minute, with which in the main I disagree, but which certainly puts forward some very strong objections, of which account must be taken. I refer particularly to what he says about the scarcity of population, and the reasons which make it unsafe to reckon upon the continuance of the high rate of profit which railways in the Gold Coast have hitherto shown. There may be an answer to these criticisms, but they deserve careful consideration.
>
> The despatch should point out that it is impossible for us to commit ourselves to a loan of any particular amount until we have the Governor's considered estimate of the further debt-charge which the Colony can bear, allowing for the inevitable increase of administrative expenditure, and taking account of the loss of revenue which will result from our liquor policy,[8] to which I see no reference in his or Mr Slater's despatches and until we know the result of the inquiries we are about to make as to the prospects of raising a loan of millions at once on the market. It would facilitate an early decision, if the Governor in his reply could contemplate the alternatives of a loan of 4 or 6 millions, and tell us, to which

8. The importing of rum from Cuba was also in process of being prohibited – an additional blow to the economy because of loss of import duty.

of the projected works he would give priority in case the lesser sum were all that was immediately obtainable. I assume that in any programme the reconstruction of the Seccondee-Coomassie line, about the urgency of which everybody seems to be agreed and which ought in any case to be undertaken without delay, will occupy the first place.

Finally I would ask the Governor what he proposes to do about the Public Works – other than transportation – a reproductive form of expenditure – which Mr Slater in his despatch of 15th July puts, if I remember rightly, at about £1,300,000. Most of these are certainly urgent, though some may possibly be postponed owing to the paramount claims of transportation. It may be that the Governor counts upon being able to provide for them out of Revenue, and there is certainly something to be said for devoting any loan that may be raised entirely to transportation – and devoting any surplus revenue to necessary but unremunerative public works. But in any case the point should be cleared up.

10 Oct. '19

Lord Milner's opening paragraph, particularly its fourth sentence, provided a masterful defusing of a potential confrontation between the new Governor and the Colonial Office. At a stroke their conflicting views were united in a practical solution. The peoples of the Gold Coast Colony owed much more than they knew to Lord Milner for his support of their more obvious champion, General Guggisberg.

It appears unnecessary to record here the full details of the despatch of 21 October, but some of the major points, apart from those just mentioned, in Milner's memo deserve comment. Much of the document was concerned with the financial aspects of transport and of other public works, although Guggisberg had not discussed the latter in his report.

Estimates for the next four years, based on a partial revision of the Acting Governor's despatch of 15 July are now shown:

Public Works[9]

Telephones and Telegraphs	£80,000
Major Public Works (Including a new hospital in Accra and a new central prison)	£1,038,000
Minor Public Works	£280,000
War Contribution to Imperial Government	£80,000
Subtotal of Public Works	£1,478,000

Total: Public Works and Transport Projects

General Public Works	£1,478,000
Roads	£500,000
Railways	£4,181,000
Harbour	£2,000,000
Grand Total for Four Years	£8,159,000

The despatch advised that the Governor should concentrate on these first four years and not undertake the wider expansion of the rail system (especially the Northern Kumasi to Gambaga extension) which with upkeep of the permanent way could total approximately £10,000,000.

An estimate of surplus of revenue over general expenditure in the Colony per annum for the next four years was £500,000 but this was subject to many variables, particularly the cocoa trade.

---

9. These figures are all in sterling, although in many of the documents the cedi (¢) is used in parallel or as an alternative.

Finally, all these aspects had to be taken into account in relation to the proposed loan of £4,000,000 or £6,000,000 and the Governor should indicate which scheme should be delayed if only the smaller sum could be raised.

Apart from his main plans, as outlined in his 'Preliminary Report', Guggisberg involved the secretariat of the Colonial Office in a welter of correspondence about appointments necessary for the implementation of these plans and for other aspects of the post-war recovery of the Colony. Thus, the appointment of surveyors for the Deep-Water Harbour Project was urgently required. The choice of Stewart and McDonnell was made for this and the contract had to be arranged through the Crown Agents (under Sir William Mercer). The firm of Stewart and McDonnell was a Canadian civil engineering partnership with experience of harbour and railway works in Canada, but had also worked with Guggisberg in France and was now based in London. Lord Milner's approval was sought and given for the establishment of two new administrative posts in Accra – Secretary and Assistant Secretary for Works, which were required to ease the growing burden on the Colonial Secretary (Mr A.R. Slater) and the Director of Public Works. Guggisberg had already chosen who should fill these posts – Mr C.W. Pettit, the then Deputy Director of Public Works in Accra, to be Secretary and Captain H.J. Gwyther MC as Assistant Secretary. (Gwyther was then acting as Brigade Major in the 100th Infantry Brigade in France, was a professional civil engineer and had served under Guggisberg on the Western Front.) Captain Gwyther's release had to be negotiated with the War Office at a high administrative level.

These appointments had Guggisberg's personal touch, something which became more and more a part of his Governorship, for he was said to have a remarkable personal knowledge of every European in the 'Coast', as well as of many Africans. Indeed it was said that, in relation to a later appointment to the Colony, other things being equal, he would like the appointee to be a good left-arm spin bowler; cricket was still a passion! And, finally, before he left England he made arrangements for the appointments of the chief commissioners to Ashanti and to the Northern Territory and for the expansion of the Department of Forestry in the Colony. The Colonial Office was probably relieved that he was now on the high seas.

Chapter XVII

COMING HOME TO CHRISTIANSBORG

The first time Gordon and Decima stayed in
Christiansborg Castle they were temporary guests of the
Acting Governor Major Herbert Bryan and his wife, but now
they took up residence by right in the picturesque old fort.
In a sense they had come home, but, sadly, they never really
had a permanent home of their own. The reader may recall
that Ellis, the Principal Clerk at the Colonial Office had
suggested that Guggisberg should not have submitted his
plans for transport 'until he had arrived in the Colony and
there considered the problem nearer at hand and at greater
leisure!' But although Guggisberg enjoyed and was a strong
advocate of active physical recreation, the word 'leisure' was
not in his vocabulary and from the day he landed, the pace at
which he drove himself and his staff was relentless.

This pace must have been particularly hard for Mr A.R.
(later Sir Ransford) Slater, the Colonial Secretary. Apart from
his own arduous administrative responsibilities, he had twice
served as Acting Governor during Sir Hugh Clifford's
absences from the Gold Coast and also during the
interregnum, when he had many problems to deal with in
the aftermath of the War. In a private letter to one of the
permanent under-secretaries at the Colonial Office, he

85

Christiansborg Castle. Guggisberg's headquarters when
Governor. Now the Presidential Residence and Seat of the
Ghana Government.

pointed out that he had been considerably out of pocket
fulfilling many special social duties on a Secretary's, *not* a
Governor's salary. Both Guggisberg and Milner supported
his receiving a Governor's salary for the whole of this
interregnum. Slater may well have been disappointed that he
was not made Governor in 1919, but to his credit, he
continued to serve Guggisberg as well as he had Clifford and
played a large part in the success of Guggisberg's ventures.
(He succeeded him as Governor.)

Guggisberg lost no time in letting the people of the Colony
know of his hopes and plans for their betterment. Although
he realized that he had to have the support of the Colonial
Office to implement them and was advised to concentrate his
efforts on the first four years, he used the occasion of his first

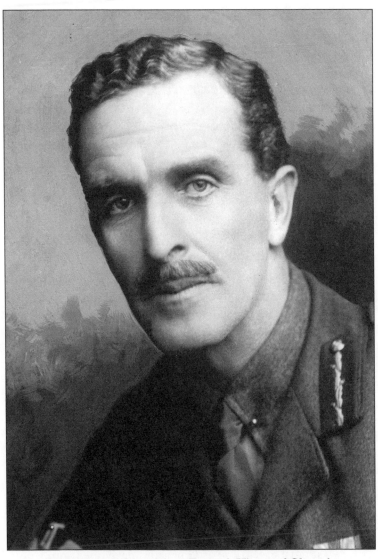

Guggisberg in his prime. (From *A History of Ghana* by
W.E.F. Ward.) Photograph by Elliott and Fry, London.
Reproduced by courtesy of the National Portrait Gallery, London.

address to the Legislative Council, only a few days after arriving in Accra to make his views public.

Whatever decisions I may be called upon to make I promise the people of the Gold Coast that I will always be guided by the fact that I am an Engineer, sent out here to superintend the construction of a broad Highway of Progress along which the races of the Gold Coast may advance by gentle gradients over the Ridges of Difficulty and by easy curves around the Swamps of Doubt and Superstition, to those far-off Cities of Promise – the Cities of Final Development, Wealth and Happiness.

As Wraith so aptly remarks, this would appear to have been composed under the influence of the Pilgrim's Progress.

About the same time an apparently minor incident occurred which may have had major consequences for the unique relationship between Governor and governed. In the service of the English Church Mission it was arranged that Guggisberg should be the first to receive Communion, but when the time came he sat in his pew and allowed the Africans to go first and then joined them. He thereby showed that in the presence of God all men are equal. It was not until after Guggisberg's death that this episode was documented and is quoted by Kimble in *A Political History of Ghana* from a speech by Glover-Addo in Legislative Council Debates, 19 June 1930.

This would appear an appropriate place to describe briefly the structure and functions of the Legislative Council, which had, by Guggisberg's time as Governor, developed into a very useful instrument of government.

The Legislative Council comprised over twenty members:

the Governor; the Colonial Secretary; the Attorney-General; the Secretary for Works;[1] the Chief Commissioners of the Regions; the Secretary for Native Affairs; the Directors of the following Departments: Public Works, Customs, Forestry, Agriculture, Post-Office and Telegraphs, Police, Surveys, Mines, Medical and Sanitary Services, Education; three representative members of the traditional chiefs; three Africans appointed from the intelligentsia; and two members from commerce.

The Council's main function was to act as an advisory body to the Governor, to debate controversial issues, to pass legislation and to initiate and receive annual and special reports from the chief commissioners of the regions, from the specialist departments and on specific topics from ad hoc committees. When the Governor and the Council disagreed on a course of action, the Governor's decision was supreme.

The Governor usually chaired the Council and in his absence the Colonial Secretary deputized as Chairman. The Governor also presented the Colony's Annual Budget and the Annual Report to the Legislative Council.

Guggisberg's Annual Report came to resemble the report of a headmaster (in some ways he was a headmaster manqué). The occasion was looked upon as the prize-giving day (or rather days!), when special praise was given to star 'pupils'. The 'Report' ran to several hundred items and members were expected to sit through it from beginning to end in the humid heat. The Governor sipped a little water, while he read every word of his 'Report'. The members sat soaked

---

1. New Post

The Legislative Council in 1919.

From left to right, seated: Dr B.W. Quartey-Papafio, H.M. Lewis (Treasurer), Togbui Sri II (Fia of Awunaga), A.R. Slater (Colonial Secretary), Nana Ofori Atta (Omanhene of Akim Abuakwa), Brigadier-General F.G. Guggisberg (Governor), Nana Amonoo V (Omanhene of Anomabu), R.W. Wilkinson (Acting Attorney-General), E.J.P. Brown, Dr D. Alexander (Acting Principal Medical Officer), Lt.-Colonel C. Harding (Commissioner of Eastern Province).

Standing: C.W. Welman (Acting Clerk of the Legislative Council), J.E. Casely Hayford, J.T. Furley (Secretary for Native Affairs), E.H.D. Nicolls (Director of Public Works), J.L. Atterbury (Acting Commissioner of Central Province), Captain P. Jeffs (Governor's Private Secretary), C.W. Pettit (Secretary for Works), H.E.G. Bartlett (Acting Commissioner of Western Province), J.I. Lauder (Acting Comptroller of Customs), F. Dawbarn.

(From Wraith's *Guggisberg*.) Published by kind permission of Oxford University Press.

with sweat, but internally dry! Yet, such was Guggisberg's charisma that no one complained.

Although African welfare and opinion were competently brought to the attention of the Administration by local chiefs and intellectuals, there was no democratic representation until several years into Guggisberg's 'reign', when he introduced the first modest changes in that direction.

But let's return to 1919 and Guggisberg's first Budget Speech.

Chapter XVIII

THE TEN-YEAR
DEVELOPMENT PROGRAMME

Guggisberg presented his long-term plans to the Legislative Council at the Budget Session on 17 November 1919, only three months after his appointment as Governor and only one month after arriving in Accra. The reader may think, why make a fuss about a development plan, something which is now commonplace, the like of which has been presented by democratic and autocratic governments all over the world? But one must remember that, in 1919, this was an entirely original venture for a governor of a British colony. Not that that signified any dereliction of duty on the part of earlier administrators, for they and their technical advisers were relatively few in number for the serving and servicing of a large part of the world, which in many instances was only beginning to emerge from the dark ages of ignorance, superstition, poverty, famine, warfare and disease. Annexations by the British were not the result of carefully developed plans, but occurred in a haphazard way, often as a result of tentative military expeditions to protect commercial interests and personnel from native peoples or from rival European powers. The wonder is that even before the First World War such a high degree of organizational development had occurred in places like the Gold Coast and that warring factions in most colonies had been controlled, except where trouble was fomented by our 'civilized' competitors. So we should not be too critical of those devoted servants who administered the Empire, for they performed remarkably well within the limits of their political, economic and technical resources. We should rather rejoice, as did the people of the Gold Coast Colony, that a man with a new vision had emerged, one who had the ability and tenacity to accomplish much of his self-engendered ten-year task.

Much of what Guggisberg hoped to achieve is in his report to Lord Milner on transportation, with the deep-water harbour his *sine qua non* for commercial viability and thus for all his other plans for development.

Guggisberg was not the originator of the idea that such a harbour was needed. In fact he first heard of the possibility when he was on the Gold Coast Survey. Later, Sir Hugh Clifford, ably supported by Mr A.R. Slater had investigated the matter, but their intentions were thwarted by the First World War. Yet, to this day, the credit goes almost exclusively to Guggisberg. In fact its completion took the whole of his tenure as Governor and he had to struggle all the way in the face of timid hesitancy, hostile criticism and technical problems.

The need for a deep-water port, where large ships could tie up alongside, was becoming more urgent, for, despite the fact that Sekondi had a shallow harbour suitable for lighters, a large quantity of cocoa was waiting to be loaded – 10,000 tons on the beach and 15,000 tons in the town. Valuable manganese exports were also blocked and imports were in chaos. Yet, perhaps surprisingly, the main opposition to the harbour in the Council came from the Africans and the commercial members. The African members would rather have spent the available money on railways and schools, with a particular eye to developing their own districts; the views of the trading companies were complicated, part of their opposition being due to vested interests in lighterage at Sekondi and elsewhere.

However, Guggisberg would not allow them to block progress. On 3 February 1921, as soon as Stewart and McDonnell had reported their choice of location (Amanful village at Takoradi, as they thought Sekondi unsuitable for further expansion) and detailed their engineering plans, he appointed a Committee under the Colonial Secretary to investigate the scheme in depth, especially its financial aspects and to advise as to whether the Colony could sustain the costs and how best to raise the money. The Committee included relevant technical and administrative officers, representatives of mercantile interests and three Africans. The Committee had to admit that without the harbour trade could never expand, in fact it could not be sustained even at its present level. The Report, to that effect, expressed with a mixture of enthusiasm and caution, was published on 11 May 1921 and was presented to the Legislative Council on 13 May. Such was Guggisberg's drive that the report was adopted and actual construction work was started less than two years after his appointment as Governor. He never wavered in his aim, even when, a year later, a slump had set in and others wished to give up. He told them that, if they gave up now, they would be the laughing stock of the Empire!

Guggisberg when Governor. (From the *Royal Engineers Journal*.)
Brigadier-General Sir Frederick Gordon Guggisberg KCMG CMG
DSO, late RE. Supplied and kindly permitted by the Royal
Engineers Library, Brompton Barracks, Chatham.

Guggisberg's growing stature as Governor was recognised in 1922 by his award of a knighthood (KCMG).

Although political and financial support for Takoradi harbour had been secured, Guggisberg had still to cope with a series of problems with the contractors. As so often happened with novel and complicated undertakings, costs were underestimated and work fell behind schedule. The situation at Takoradi was especially complicated in that Stewart and McDonnell were advising as well as constructing. One of the main technical problems was that, because of 'imperial preference', they were not allowed to import the machinery they considered essential for the task and which was not available in Britain. Eventually they pulled out of the contract. On 18 September 1924 the firm of Sir Robert McAlpine replaced them and soon went ahead of schedule. Again, Guggisberg's nerve held through these difficulties and by now he was so highly regarded by his former critics in the Council that they unanimously accepted these major changes. (It is interesting to note, however, that one of the criticisms of Mr W.D. Ellis in 1919 had been of the dual role to which Stewart and McDonnell were to be appointed.)

Although the deep-water harbour had been the top priority of Guggisberg's plans, the complex project was not quite complete in 1927, when his appointment as Governor ended. (British Colonial Governorships were almost always of limited tenure, no matter how successful.)[1] However, Guggisberg must have been highly gratified that the ship which took him on his last voyage from the Gold Coast anchored in the shelter of the Takoradi breakwaters. The

---

1. In fact Guggisberg's eight years was double his expected four years.

Tema Harbour. This large modern port in Eastern Ghana
supplements but does not supersede Guggisberg's great harbour
at Takoradi. The photograph shows a surf boat dwarfed by a
modern cargo liner.

unkind cut was to come a year later, when, on 3 April 1928,
the harbour was officially opened by Mr J.H. Thomas, the
then Secretary of State for the Colonies, but Guggisberg,
although he would have been free to go, was not invited to
the ceremony. The only recognition of the chief architect of
the project was in the name of one of the harbour tugs – *Sir
Gordon*. The 'sister-ship' of the *Sir Gordon* was called the *Sir
Ransford* after the former Colonial Secretary, A.R. (Alexander
Ransford) Slater who had been knighted in 1925 when
Governor of Sierra Leone; as has already been pointed out,
he made an enormous contribution to the planning of the
harbour and to other aspects of the Ten-Year Development
Programme. How the snub to Guggisberg came about was

never really clear, but apparently J.H. Thomas was amazed to learn, only during his visit to the Colony, about Sir Gordon's key rôle in the construction!

In relation to the deep-water harbour we have run ahead of other aspects of the 'Ten-Year Development Programme', to which we now return.

Guggisberg's predecessors had already pioneered the development of the railways, but his personal stamps were to speed up construction and to coordinate their development with the building of the harbour and of feeder roads to the rail system. (His comprehensive overview of transport and his drive might have worked wonders for Britain itself at several important stages in development!) Behind the intensity of his speeches and actions lay the fear, which he did not hesitate to publicize, that, if its railway system did not develop at speed, the Gold Coast would be left behind in the growing general demand for cocoa products and would be beaten to world markets by Brazil and Nigeria.

Two important factors enhanced the speed and efficiency of railway development – the employment of established, experienced railway and public works staff on construction and the fact that Guggisberg, as an engineer, could understand the calculations and techniques required. Mutual respect and confidence were generated to a degree unheard of in other colonial administrations.

Of the railways in the 'Programme' the following were completed: the 'missing' part of the Accra–Kumasi line between Tafo and Kumasi was opened to trains by September 1923; the reconstruction of the Sekondi–Kumasi line was finished by October 1926; and, by 1927, eighty miles of the

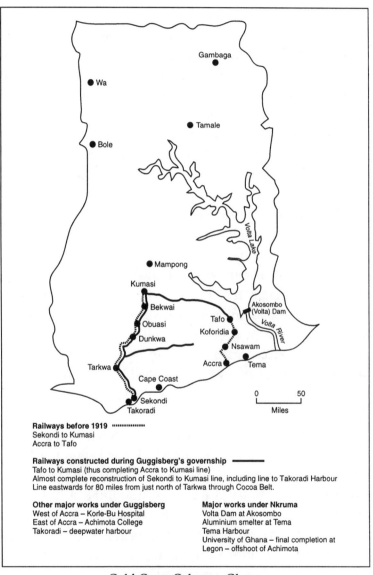

Gambaga

Wa

Tamale

Bole

Volta Lake

Mampong

Kumasi

Bekwai

Akosombo
(Volta) Dam

Obuasi

Tafo

Volta River

Dunkwa

Koforidia

Nsawam

Tarkwa

Accra

Tema

Cape Coast

0   50

Sekondi
Takoradi

Miles

Railways before 1919 ┈┈┈┈┈┈
Sekondi to Kumasi
Accra to Tafo

Railways constructed during Guggisberg's governship ────
Tafo to Kumasi (thus completing Accra to Kumasi line)
Almost complete reconstruction of Sekondi to Kumasi line, including line to Takoradi Harbour
Line eastwards for 80 miles from just north of Tarkwa through Cocoa Belt.

Other major works under Guggisberg
West of Accra – Korle-Bu Hospital
East of Accra – Achimota College
Takoradi – deepwater harbour

Major works under Nkruma
Volta Dam at Akosombo
Aluminium smelter at Tema
Tema Harbour
University of Ghana – final completion at
Legon – offshoot of Achimota

Gold Coast Colony – Ghana.
Anachronistic map of major developments.

99

link between the two main lines through the central cocoa belt were also open to traffic. The simple figures for new railway track during Guggisberg's Governorship are impressive – an expansion from 269 miles to 475 miles. Thus, including the 150 miles rebuilt between Sekondi and Kumasi, some 350 miles had been laid.

Because of the more expensive high-priority harbour and railways, roads were initially built on a simple, cheap basis – so-called 'pioneer' roads – cleared through the bush, but with only rudimentary surfaces: 'a sticky quagmire in the rains and a corrugated, pot-holed hell in the dry season', quoted from Wraith's *Guggisberg*. This temporary compromise, organized through district commissioners and local chiefs and using local labour, was encouraged so that at least the clearances through the forests were made for later, more permanent roads to link with the rail system and even in the interim the flow of goods was facilitated. The later main roads were surfaced with granite or quartzite chips, quarry dust, tar and sand and were researched by the Public Works Department under the guidance of the Governor! They cost about £1,000 a mile.

One of the most impressively engineered roads in the country is the series of bends by which one climbs the Aburi escarpment from the Accra Plains – it was made by Italian engineers. Even today roads are still a problem in Ghana, one of the main snags being that heavy rains soften and wash away the laterite earth, undermining the edges of tarred surfaces, so leading to a crumbling of the crust under the weight of heavy trucks, particularly those carrying large tree trunks.

Chapter XIX

KORLE-BU HOSPITAL

This was the first major modern hospital in tropical Africa. Although it was part of the Ten-Year Development Programme, plans for its construction were already advanced when Guggisberg became Governor. However, as with transport its concept was enhanced and building expedited by his imaginative and enthusiastic touch. It is the place where the writer first encountered the great man, or rather his statue! There is a temptation for a medical person to be expansive on health matters, but in this compact biography these must not be allowed to overshadow other aspects. (It is hoped later to write another more detailed account of medical developments.)

Korle-Bu Hospital is situated just west of Accra, beyond the lagoon and is now linked by a coastal causeway to the old part of the city. It is built on fairly flat scrubland and the site was well chosen to allow expansion, not only of hospital facilities but also of staff housing.

Guggisberg planned to use the hospital for the training of doctors, nurses, technicians and other health professionals, but it was not until Nkrumah's presidency, about forty years later, that the University of Ghana Medical School was established. Guggisberg's ambition was for the Korle-Bu complex to become the medical college for all British West Africa. He was dissatisfied with the training of doctors away from Africa and indeed, he was sure that more relevant education and training for other professions should largely be in the Colony. However, we will come to these wider aspects of education later.

Korle-Bu Hospital was not the only medical building constructed under the Ten-Year Programme, for eighteen smaller hospitals and twenty dispensaries were also completed by 1927.

It would appear that medical administrative thought in West Africa at the beginning of the twentieth century was obsessed with the not undeserved reputation of the 'Coast' as the 'White Man's Grave'; so much so that in 1912 a meeting of Principal Medical Officers in Lagos proposed to segregate Europeans from Africans. Sir Hugh Clifford vetoed that extreme form of hygienic apartheid. It was he also who initiated the planning of the major hospital at Korle-Bu and who developed waterworks for Accra and Sekondi, schemes already started by Governor Sir John Rodger.

In these days, as today, malaria was the most prevalent disease, sometimes in its potentially lethal acute forms, especially cerebral malaria and blackwater fever, sometimes in its more chronic forms with recurrent fever and persistent ill health. Although the abnormal sickle shape of red cells had been described in 1910, in an American of African descent, its frequency in West Africa and relationship to malaria had not even been dreamed of when Korle-Bu Hospital was founded. Yet traditional medicine-men were aware of the symptoms which we now know to be due to

Korle-Bu Hospital, Accra – 1. Sir Gordon Guggisberg's statue
beside the administrative block (the Author's first 'contact' with
the great governor – February 1971).

sickle-cell disease, especially the attacks of severe bone pain.
However, by the first time Guggisberg went to the Gold
Coast as a surveyor, it was known that anopheles mosquitoes
transmitted malaria and thus the use of suitable nets and the
wearing of high, soft-leather boots had been added to the
taking of quinine in preventive measures. Similarly the
transmission of sleeping sickness (trypanosome infection) by
the tsetse fly was also known. (It should be remembered that
trypanosomiasis was a relatively greater scourge of horses
and cattle than of man.) Food and water-borne infections
were common, especially typhoid fever and various types of
dysentery and Guggisberg himself would eventually die from
complications of one of the latter – amoebic infection of the
liver. Smallpox was still a scourge and leprosy endemic.

Korle-Bu Hospital, Accra – 2. The same part of the hospital under
construction in 1921, identifiable by the characteristic double
pillars. (Photograph reproduced by permission of the Keeper of
the Public Records, Kew.) Photograph supplied by the Public
Record Office, Kew, which holds the original: Ref. CO 98/34.

Yellow fever was almost certainly the most feared disease
along the coast of West Africa and in the Caribbean area.
That reputation was due to three main factors: first the
devastating severity of the illness, especially in Europeans,
with high mortality; second, the size of the epidemics,
particularly in the Spanish-American War in Cuba; and,
third, the mystery which so long surrounded its cause. Initial
fever was followed by severe liver damage with consequent
jaundice (hence the name yellow fever), vomiting of blood
and collapse (often fatal). Large epidemics occurred in dense
populations – cities and armies – the so-called urban type;
and smaller outbreaks in less developed areas – the so-called

forest or sylvan type, the latter from a reservoir of infection in monkeys. An important advance was the finding that in the urban outbreaks the disease was transmitted from man to man by aedes mosquitoes, but early research using the light-microscope failed to show a causal organism.

The reader may now be saying, 'He promised not to overemphasize medical matters and where does Guggisberg come into the story?'

It was thus: the research laboratories built by Guggisberg as part of the Korle-Bu complex played a vital part in advancing the understanding and eventual control of yellow fever for they quickly became the focal point for outstanding medical investigators. In their own way they might almost be reckoned as being in the Guggisberg mould; their pioneering work will now be briefly recalled.

Chapter XX

TRAGEDY AND TRIUMPH

Research on yellow fever reached a dramatic climax within a year of Guggisberg's leaving the Gold Coast. Simultaneous work in Accra, Lagos and London solved several problems which cleared the way towards successful prevention. But a high price was paid: three doctors died, one in Lagos and then two in Accra, from the dread disease, accidentally acquired.

Courageous work by pathologists in the United States Army had already shown that yellow fever could be transmitted experimentally to human volunteers (including themselves and some of them died) from infectious patients both by direct inoculation and by the bites of mosquitoes. The infective agent appeared to pass through a bacterial filter and was thus most likely to be a virus. Yet there was still some doubt as to whether this was a real virus or a tiny spiral organism (leptospira). The first priority of the workers in Accra and Lagos was to exclude the latter.

In order to facilitate their research and avoid the use of human volunteers, they used macaque (rhesus) monkeys for their experiments. They found these animals to be highly susceptible to very small amounts of infective material from human patients dying of the disease (tissue from the spleen or serum from the blood). All rhesus monkeys thus infected died. The man who worked mainly in the Lagos laboratory was Professor Adrian Stokes, an Irishman, professor of pathology at Guy's Hospital, London. He was chosen for this work because of his experience with leptospirosis in the trenches on the Western Front, where soldiers were infected through minor breaches in the skin by organisms from the urine of rats carrying the disease. Stokes's experiments with the monkeys and his co-operation with the Accra workers on the exclusion of leptospira infection came to an abrupt end on 19 September 1927, when he died of yellow fever, almost certainly the result of a bite by one of his own mosquitoes. Work continued apace in the Gold Coast and the possibility of a leptospira as the cause of yellow fever was finally excluded.

Three men were involved in this work – W.A. (Bill) Young, Hideyo Noguchi and Percy (later Sir Percy) Selwyn-Clarke. All three were unique characters.

Young was a Scot who qualified in medicine at the Dundee Medical School (a St Andrews graduate) and early in life dedicated himself to tropical medicine. He was appointed pathologist and director of medical research in the new Korle-Bu laboratories. From his earlier researches Young favoured a viral cause of yellow fever.

Despite his own opinions, Young welcomed Noguchi to his laboratory to give the leptospira possibility a fair trial. Professor Noguchi was born in Japan, but emigrated to America and eventually joined the Rockefeller Institute. He became a world authority on the spiral-shaped organisms of syphilis, relapsing fever and leptospirosis and no one was

Korle-Bu Hospital, Accra – 3. Research laboratory building in
which Noguchi and Young worked on yellow fever.

better qualified to investigate this aspect of yellow fever.
Although he and Young had differing views on the disease
they were firm friends.

Selwyn-Clarke investigated the clinical and epidemio-
logical features of an outbreak of yellow fever in Accra from
which the laboratory workers derived their specimens.
(Selwyn-Clarke later became famous as the chief medical
officer in Hong Kong during the Japanese occupation, when
he defied the military authorities and probably only survived
because a Japanese medical officer knew of his work on
yellow fever!)

The results of the research were disappointing for
Noguchi, but a vindication of Young's views. Sadly just as
the work was being completed, Noguchi contracted yellow
fever. He died on 21 May 1928. Young did not shirk the

108

unpleasant and dangerous task of doing a post-mortem examination on his friend and embalming him.

He died of the same infection on 30 May.

The British Medical Journal of 9 June 1928 contained Young's obituary. It also published a paper by Dr Edward Hindle, a Beit Memorial Research Fellow of the Wellcome Bureau of Scientific Research, on 'A Yellow Fever Vaccine'. This described the first successful protection of rhesus monkeys from yellow fever by a formalinized vaccine and soon led to human vaccination against the disease. Sadly it came too late for Stokes, Noguchi and Young.

Yet these were merely the first steps towards a healthier nation. The reputation of the 'Coast' as the 'White Man's Grave' has already been mentioned, but it could equally well have been described as the 'Black Child's Grave'.

Infant and maternal mortality were unacceptably high and Guggisberg and his medical advisers were in no doubt as to the urgent need for maternity services, infant welfare and improved nutrition.

In the seventy years since he left Accra, his dream of a medical school there has been amply fulfilled; a second school in Kumasi has just celebrated its coming of age; and a third, in Tamale, has been founded. But the nature of the human condition and the hostile environment of West Africa are such that hopes of lasting solutions are dashed. For the solving of old problems is countered by the emergence of new ones, as in the AIDS pandemic, the increasing resistance of malaria parasites to drugs and the spread of bilharzia in the wake of irrigation. The optimism of Guggisberg that the pilgrimage would attain eventual success has been replaced by the reality of a continuing struggle, bafflingly complex and so costly as to require the support of the World Health Organisation.

Chapter XXI

FARMING AND FORESTRY

We have diverted a little from our main theme. Yet, even in that diversion, we have seen how Guggisberg's concentration on what is now called infrastructure, specifically in relation to the research laboratories at Korle-Bu, was not long in advancing the health of the colony, an advance of worldwide importance. However, his main thrust was to provide transport for the exports which were to pay for better and more universally available education. By then, cocoa was the most valuable export, greater even than gold.

Cocoa is the product of the cacao tree, a small evergreen of tropical American origin (*Theobroma cacao*). Its seed-pods contain the beans from which cocoa powder and chocolate are prepared. The tree was brought indirectly to the Gold Coast Colony via the island of Fernando Po in the Gulf of Guinea, by Tetteh Quarshie, who had been working on the island and took the seed-pods home. (Some twenty years earlier Basel missionaries had unsuccessfully attempted to establish seedlings.) Thus the introduction and basic production of cocoa owed nothing to the British.

The warm, moist climate and shady glades of the southern part of Ashanti and the Western and Central Regions of the Gold Coast proved to be ideal for the cultivation of cacao

111

trees, which were efficiently managed by small farmers. As business expanded they formed co-operatives and Guggisberg encouraged this, for he was keen that middlemen should not take too much of the profit.

Production of cocoa grew at an amazing rate: thus, in 1891, 80lb of cocoa were exported from the Gold Coast and in 1931, 300,000 tons. In fact there was a steady increase between these years. The following table of Quinquennial Averages illustrates the expansion:

Years	5-Year Annual Average in Tons
1891-95	5
1896-1900	230
1901-05	3,172
1906-10	14,784
1911-15	51,819
1916-20	106,072
1921-25	186,320
1926-30	218,895

(Figures from Bourret, *Ghana – The Road to Independence*, 1960. Permission of Oxford University Press.)

The expansion was all the more creditable because it did not receive any influx of European capital.

Guggisberg was naturally delighted that the cocoa industry was in such a thriving state, but there were worries. Slumps in the industrial world caused serious falls in the price of cocoa e.g. from about £50 per ton in a 'good' year to about half the value. Disappointed growers might be tempted to curtail production and switch to another crop. Guggisberg thought that the Colony should not rely on a single crop for its prosperity. He warned the chiefs and farmers how risky it was to base the economy on the whims of the British housewife and her liking for cocoa and chocolate. Yet cocoa did bring a raised standard of living to the peasant farmers and duty on its export value (ranging from 12 per cent to 28 per cent) provided useful revenue for many important projects. Africans hated direct taxation on income, but grudgingly tolerated the cocoa export levy. However it was pointed out that total annual indirect taxation per head of population in the Colony was 16 shillings, whereas in the UK the tax burden was £23 per head.

As Takoradi harbour neared completion, Guggisberg's enthusiasm grew for an expansion in the range of agricultural exports. He had a vision of ships laden with palm oil, shea butter and groundnuts, but he could not prevail upon the farmers to cultivate more widely and intensively with a view to export. One particular dis-appointment was in relation to sisal: he was keen that this source of coarse fibre should be grown on a large scale on the Accra plains; but he failed to force the pace for this radical innovation. In fact only the palm oil business has continued, although earlier restricted by imperial embargo and export duty, and later by the making of palm wine.

As he mentioned in his 'Preliminary Report on Transportation', Guggisberg was concerned about the existence of 'meat famine' and hoped that it would be alleviated by the development of the Northern Territories for cattle rearing, but neither that nor the northern extension of the railway was achieved. (Modest progress in the rearing of cattle has been made more recently.)

In fact the supply of first-class protein is still a problem today. Hens and goats are to be found in most villages and towns and there are a few pig farms. There is an experimental farm for milk production on the campus of the University of Science and Technology (UST) Kumasi, using Canadian Holstein cows.

Inshore fishing along the coast is very important, although still using the same type of surf boats which were used to land the Guggisbergs ninety years ago.

But the main message about Sir Gordon's drive for food production is the breadth of his knowledge of local products and his vision as to how they should be developed.

Forests have an indirect importance in cocoa production, because their damp shade provides ideal conditions for the cacao trees. But that was only one aspect of the functions of the Forestry Department.

Government input to forestry was in abeyance for most of the First World War (with the exception of a part-time watching brief by one officer). However, about the time that Guggisberg became Governor, the Conservator of Forests (N.C. McLeod) returned to duty and, supported by new assistants, pursued a vigorous and enlightened policy. In the 'Report of the Forestry Department for 1920' to the Legislative Council he expressed optimism for the future, provided that the Chiefs, the Political Officers and the Forestry Officers worked together for long-term balance between utilization and conservation. If necessary there must be legal enforcement, for, in the past, promises by chiefs had not been fulfilled, setting aside at one stage only 240 square miles instead of the 6,000 square miles needed. This was a thorny problem because of long-standing ordinances to protect the natives from takeover or exploitation of such valuable lands. However by 1927 it was necessary to get the Attorney-General to introduce legislation to ensure conservation and it was pointed out that the directive involved changes in the *use* of the forest lands, not in their ownership.

Biologically there were several problems. Too much production of cocoa depleted large areas of the necessary forest shade and made early reafforestation unlikely. The lifespan of cacao trees (less than twenty years) was also important in this respect. What McLeod referred to as 'Cocoa mania' was also causing great damage to the rubber industry, because farmers were too busy with cocoa to tap the rubber trees. Finally, the future production of high-quality, mahogany-type hardwoods was dependent on the careful long-term management of surviving forests, because the cutting down of such a valuable resource was proceeding at excessive speed.

(All commendably '*green*'!)

The more one examines the records of the Legislative Council and the departmental support for its deliberations, the more is one impressed by the ability, energy and dedication of the technical and administrative personnel – often functioning in a far from ideal environment.

Chapter XXII

THE ULTIMATE OBJECTIVE

Guggisberg's eventual aim was to liberate the Africans of the Gold Coast Colony by education, enabling them to attain a level of civilization equivalent to that of Europeans. He was in no doubt as to their intellectual potential. All other activities and achievements were simply means to the educational end. His thoughts, words and deeds in relation to education must therefore be examined in considerable detail.

For the sake of clarity these will be considered under five headings:

1. Official Reports to the Legislative Council.
2. The Planning, Building and Manning of Achimota College.
3. *The Keystone* – Guggisberg's small book on his educational aims.
4. The Visit to America.
5. *The Future of the Negro* – a book jointly written by Sir Gordon and the Rev. A.G. Fraser.

THE ULTIMATE OBJECTIVE

Official Reports to the Legislative Council on Education

Two separate committees to report on education were appointed in rapid succession: the first in 1919 by Clifford; the second in 1920 by Guggisberg. We will concern ourselves with the facts and not speculate on the motives behind these moves. The 'Clifford Committee' had twelve (plus two extra) members, mainly from the Legislative Council, four men of the cloth and the Director of Education (D.J. Oman) who also acted as Secretary. From 14 July until 19 September they met seven times, under the Chairmanship of the Acting Colonial Secretary (D. Kingdon). Their report was only eleven pages in length; it cost two shillings.

They recommended that the following be adopted in the sequence indicated:

1. An amendment of Education Rates and Schedules.
2. The establishment in the neighbourhood of Accra of a Government Secondary School for boys, to be known as 'The Royal College, Accra' and the erection, as part of such a college of a Natural Science Laboratory to be built with the Cadbury Gift (this was of £5,000). All pupils would be boarders; they would total 100.
3. The establishment of a Government Primary School for Girls at Seccondee.
4. The establishment of a Secondary Government Boarding School for girls in the neighbourhood of Accra (total 100).
5. The establishment of additional technical schools at Cape Coast, Seccondee and Coomassie.
6. The establishment, if found necessary, of a Government

117

Boarding School for boys, preparatory for the 'Royal College'.

7. The establishment of industrial schools.

This compact report was presented to Guggisberg, but was not directly acted upon, because he had a much fuller personal agenda on the matter.

He appointed a second committee to advise on 'Educational Matters'. The 'Guggisberg Committee' was chaired by the Director of Education, had only six members, but took evidence from Legislative Councillors and various experts (twelve oral and four written submissions). It also considered, in no small measure, the Governor's speech to the Legislative Council on 23 February 1920, the Report of the 'Clifford Committee' and several other documents. The 'Guggisberg Committee' was appointed on *5 March 1920* and *reported on 22 May 1920*.

They met *42* times. Their report was of approximately 100 pages; it cost (only) 3 shillings; it contained *334* paragraphs and included *52* Recommendations.

At first sight, this second report might seem excessive, but it is not just a general report with a few specific recommendations, it is an entire blueprint for revolutionizing education in the Gold Coast, for all ages, both sexes, academic high-fliers and technical trainees. It explores the relationship between government and mission education and sets out developments over the next decade. Nor does it omit to address financial implications. The Governor obviously had a powerful guiding hand in the committee's work – the report had an important postscript.

'P.S. Your Excellency has intimated that the Report will be

taken home "for further conference with the Colonial Office and with the leaders of the British Educational World". The members of your Committee, Sir, would be honoured if it could be arranged that the Director of Education, their Chairman, could represent them at such a Conference to supply the detailed information which will be required.' (They obviously felt strongly that the Governor's amateur enthusiasm should be balanced by professional realism.)

One of the main resolutions was to establish a complex residential college for both sexes near Achimota just east of Accra. This is of such importance as to justify separate study.

Achimota College

The establishment of this college was a much more ambitious scheme than that of 'The Royal College, Accra', in scope of educational content, range of age, 'catering' for both sexes and aiming for much larger numbers. To some extent it changed and developed along the way, for it existed primarily in the fertile imagination of the Governor (relatively an amateur) and not in the professionally structured plans of experts in education, who were obliged to follow what to them were somewhat whimsical ideas and ideals. But, as with Takoradi harbour, Guggisberg won through.

The first breakthrough for the Governor in relation to the support of professionals for his ideas on education came from an unexpected quarter. When he was in London in 1920, visiting the Colonial Office with his plans for education, including the building of an advanced institute at Achimota, he had the good fortune to meet members of the Phelps-Stokes Commission on Education. This was founded by a trust set up with money bequeathed by a wealthy American lady, Miss Caroline Phelps-Stokes, to help with the education of Negroes and American Indians in the United States and later in other parts of the world, including an extensive fact-finding itinerary in Africa. They and Guggisberg were thrilled to find that many of their ideas on the education of Africans coincided. They were particularly involved with the educational initiatives at Hampton, Virginia and Tuskegee, Alabama, which we will discuss later. In addition to the general boost to his own crusade, Guggisberg met Dr J.E.K. Aggrey, a native of the Gold Coast, who had lived in USA for twenty years and was probably the most influential member of the Commission. In London and aboard ship on the voyage back to the 'Coast', Aggrey and Guggisberg became firm friends and eventually Aggrey was persuaded to return home and join the staff of the new college at Achimota.

Dr Aggrey was an outgoing, friendly man, but an intellectual giant, a born teacher, a polymath and a devout Christian preacher – the ideal person that General Guggisberg was looking for to implement his schemes for education. And it should also be emphasized that Aggrey was the man who persuaded the Governor of the supreme importance of full education for girls!

Despite the fact that Guggisberg now had influential supporters, he still had opposition from a wide range of critics in the Gold Coast: the Europeans were sceptical of the whole idea of a costly college which would embrace kindergarten, preparatory, English-type public school and university levels of education, with one of the main notions of training teachers to act as leaven for the expansion of education throughout the Colony; the expatriates also accused the Governor of sentimentality or of cynically courting popularity with the natives; some of the British feared for their jobs and loss of influence with an increase in the number of Africans who could replace them; a local newspaper, the *Gold Coast Independent* attacked the idea of higher education in Africa as it would eliminate the need for education in Britain, one of the main stepping-stones to status and success. The Governor was also accused of paternalism, especially in relation to his emphasis on vocational training, which his accusers said was a mechanism for restricting the African to more menial occupations. However, by now the Governor had the full backing of the Chiefs and other Africans in the Legislative Council.

Guggisberg steamed ahead; in May 1922 he appointed yet another committee. This was really a planning committee to work out the details of the building of Achimota College to the Governor's own specifications! The committee was presented with a Memorandum as to his wishes and this was supplemented by drawings from a Cambridge architect (a Major Skipper) with the advice, 'Major Skipper's lay-out is excellent and will be adhered to.' Needless to say the vice-regal engineer's plans were accepted!

Guggisberg laid the Foundation Stone of the College in March 1924.

The planning committee were asked to give their views as to how it would be possible to reconcile general secondary education, teacher training, technical education, professional education and the association of both sexes within one boarding establishment! (Not unexpectedly, missionaries and the more conservative African leaders were not in favour of the last proposal.) The Governor was also keen that the College should expand upward to become a University. Finally, in relation to the grand design of Achimota, the College was to become an administratively and financially independent organization with the status of a special department of the Government and in the hands of a headmaster responsible to the Governor. The kindly and considerate Mr Wraith in his detailed and sensitive appraisal of what that meant to the Department of Education is worthy of full quotation.

> The Director of Education, D.J. Oman, was a patient and much tried man. From the moment of Guggisberg's arrival in the Colony he had been harassed, overworked and put upon; he served the Governor faithfully, and his reward was to see his authority and that of his staff constantly eroded by Guggisberg's direct interventions, and finally to have the College taken out of his hands. He is one of the unsung heroes of the Guggisberg revolution, but it casts no slur on his memory to say that these things could not have been achieved under his leadership. He was a good servant and a willing horse on whom an accident of history had launched a human dynamo. He and his colleagues would have been less than human if they had not occasionally resented it.[1]

---

1. Mr Oman must have had considerable physical stamina and a robust personality, because, having survived eight years of Guggisberg's reign, he became the first District Grand Master of the English Freemasons in the Gold Coast from 1931 to 1936. (Related to the writer by a close Ghanaian friend.)

Even when the building of the school was under construction, Guggisberg kept checking on progress, particularly on how well the contractors were performing. The school is only a few miles from Christiansborg Castle and he visited it three times a week when resident there.

Eventually, as with Takoradi harbour, the initial contractor withdrew and Achimota College was completed by the Public Works Department. One bone of contention during construction was the cost of the clock tower which the Governor insisted was essential.

So much for the bricks and mortar! What of the teaching staff? Here Guggisberg met his match in the two leaders of the school – Rev. A.G. Fraser and Dr J.E.K. Aggrey. Both were of high international reputation and both were to be the subject of dedicated biographies. Guggisberg knew of Fraser by reputation as the successful Principal of Trinity College, Kandy, Ceylon. Fraser was a fiery, non-conformist Scot and, though he shared many of Guggisberg's views on education, quarrelled with him on several occasions; he became Principal of Achimota College. Aggrey was a much more placid man, despite the racist insults he had received and indeed his appointment as Assistant Vice-Principal was in itself a sop to racial prejudice, as the authorities were unwilling to have an African in the potential position of officially running the College in Fraser's absence. Fortunately for the school the benign and magnanimous Dr Aggrey accepted the flawed appointment, being only interested in helping the youth of his country. The other two members of the Achimota triumvirate, Guggisberg and Fraser do not come well out of this treatment of their close colleague.

Although Guggisberg was keen that Christian virtues should have a part to play in character building, he was not an articulate advocate of these and, when the Anglican bishop of Accra tried to build a kind of religious apartheid of Achimota Anglicans and others, he needed the resolute Fraser to help him reject the idea.

In fact Fraser came into Guggisberg's life when he was beginning to give more thought to spiritual matters. Wraith tells of an amazing dialogue between them in a street in Accra. Guggisberg took exception to the fact that the Principal of his great College often went around in shorts. One day when being driven in downtown Accra he spotted him thus attired and had his chauffeur stop the car to remonstrate with him. Fraser replied that they were good for gardening, were respectable and acceptable to God. Guggisberg indicated that religion and God meant nothing to him, but finished the confrontation by promising Fraser that he would, from that day, spend ten minutes in every twenty-four hours communing with his Maker! Such was the calibre of the founders of Achimota.

In October 1924, Fraser, Aggrey and four members of staff started work, so that when the College was finally opened in 1927 every detail would be meticulously prepared and recruiting of pupils organized. The kindergarten and teacher's training sections were established and staff were intensively instructed in local languages and customs.

The Prince of Wales visited the establishment in April 1925 and agreed that the main school take his name. (This was later dropped, after his abdication.)

We will jump ahead of our narrative briefly to record the

The Official Opening of Achimota. (From Wraith's *Guggisberg*, 1967. Permission of Oxford University Press.)

official opening of the College on 27 January 1927 and the sudden, sad death of Aggrey six months later.

Guggisberg himself performed the opening ceremony and a great occasion it was, with the beating of drums, the blowing of horns, the assembled colourful finery of the chiefs, including the Asantehene (only three years back from exile in the Seychelles) and the formal stiff white collars and black suits of the legal profession – 'the greatest day in the history of the Gold Coast'.

Dr Aggrey went to New York to write a book to submit for the PhD of Columbia University, but took ill after writing only a few pages and quickly died. His death was not just a personal tragedy for his family and his many friends; it was a sad, devastating blow to the future of the country to lose such a wonderful leader. He had an amazingly tolerant outlook on the problem of colour prejudice and, when quite a young man spoke the Parable of the Piano Keys. 'You can play a tune of sorts on the white keys, and you can play a tune of sorts on the black keys, but for harmony you must use both the black and white.'

After Aggrey's death, Fraser had the black and white keys worked into a design for the emblem of the school – the Black and White Shield of Achimota.

The Keystone

This small publication, the germ of Guggisberg's thoughts and actions on education, was written at sea on board SS *Ada*, sailing from the Gold Coast to England in April 1924. He had just laid the foundation stone of the College at Achimota and, as he so often did, he gives an update of the current position of education and sets out his aims for its future in the Gold Coast Colony.

His words now follow and begin with his own simple drawing.

THE KEYSTONE

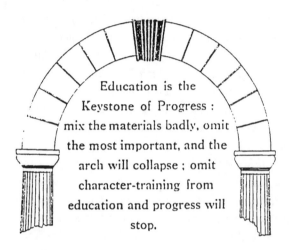

Education is the Keystone of Progress : mix the materials badly, omit the most important, and the arch will collapse ; omit character-training from education and progress will stop.

By

BRIGADIER-GENERAL SIR GORDON GUGGISBERG,

K.C.M.G., D.S.O., late R.E.

1924.
SIMPKIN, MARSHALL, HAMILTON, KENT & CO. LTD.,
LONDON, E.C. 4.

FOREWORD

The Book of Education of the Gold Coast has yet to be written; this is a mere booklet describing the present situation with regard to education and attempting to paint the picture of the future. My only excuse for writing it is that some of my African friends have asked me to do so; they say, with justice, that I have spoken much on the subject in public, but that the spoken word does not reach the many literate Africans who are scattered through the 'far, far bush' of a country that is greater in area than England, Scotland and Wales. My friends assure me that, if Government's plans for education were better known, there would be better cooperation with the people. As this is essential to the future well-being of the country, I accept their assurance.

Hence this booklet. It is disjointed and scrappy. It cannot be complete because, as I shall presently show, we are at the parting of the ways, at a point in our narrow old main road where a wide new thoroughfare is being surveyed and staked out across the flat 'Plains of Elementary Education' towards the 'Hill of Higher Education' – Achimota. But anyway it may show what Government is doing while that thoroughfare is building and may indicate the direction of all the little roads that are being planned to connect up our educational system.

When the whole system is planned and made known, I think that a number of keen young Africans in the Government service who have had no chance of obtaining a higher education will find that they have not been forgotten. There will be opportunities of entering Achimota for those who have given real promise.

It goes without saying that anything I write in this booklet applies to the Gold Coast and nowhere else; my remarks on the 'African' apply to the 'Gold Coast African'. The races of Africa are in such varying stages of development that some of them have by no means reached the point on the Road of Progress at which a higher education is either within their intellectual grasp or would be good for their future. In the Gold Coast itself – the Colony, Ashanti and the Northern Territories – conditions vary so greatly as to necessitate caution in the application of the principles advocated in this booklet. The moment for reviewing the educational situation is a proper one. We have just laid the foundation stone of Achimota College, an institution that is destined to be the mainspring of all educational works in this country. While the walls of the College are slowly rising from the ground a staff of picked men will gradually be gathered together; a definite scheme will be drawn up for progressive education from the infant school to the university or the workshop; the needs of the country will be carefully considered; and on all these things will be based the future curriculum of Achimota.

I confess that, as I stood on the platform on the barren hill-top of Achimota on the 24th March, 1924, and looked round the great horse-shoe of spectators, I was deeply impressed by the importance of the occasion that had brought us together. I had just passed through two long lines of Boy Scouts, their faces and their bearing showing that 'B P.'s' great system of character-training was already taking effect; just inspected the Guard of Honour of the Gold Coast Regiment, hardy fighting men from the far North whose breasts carried evidence of their readiness to defend their country against aggression, whose education for the moment is limited to that of discipline and self-sacrifice, but for whom greater benefits lie hidden in the distant future. To my right in the horse-shoe were those who had inherited for many generations the qualities conferred on them by the education of their forbears, the number of these Europeans, the distance from which they had come, and the nature of the occasion, testifying that they at all events were not of those who disbelieved in the education of the African. Scattered thickly among them were the European-clad Africans – barristers, doctors, teachers, traders – the pioneers of the progress of their race, their faces ample proof of their satisfaction that, at long last, the dream they had dreamed was approaching realisation. To the left were many Chiefs in their robes and insignia of State, surrounded by their Councillors and sword bearers, their attitude leaving no doubt in one's mind but that they shared with their countrymen the appreciation of what was coming.

I was assisted in laying the foundation-stone by African professional men: we shared in the manual labour. All had received their higher education in Europe: only two professions could supply properly qualified members – engineering, for example, was symbolised by a boy mechanic. Scathing comment on the inadequacy of our existing system of education.

The stone that we laid marks the end of the old system; the new will begin with the opening of the college on the 1st January, 1927. May the blessing given by the Bishop of Accra on that block of concrete spread, like a creeper from its roots, over the whole of Achimota and help it in turn to lay the foundation of the New Era in the Gold Coast.

THE KEYSTONE
CHAPTER I
NECESSITY FOR BETTER EDUCATION
OF THE AFRICAN

Wherever one turns in the Gold Coast one meets the same demand – a better education for Africans than our present schools are capable of providing. Apart from the fact that the people themselves are clamouring for a better education, the future of the country demands it. In the Government Service alone the need is urgent; the development of the country is progressing so rapidly that we can no longer afford the proportionately larger number of Europeans required to deal with the work for their long leave, their steamer-passages, and the higher rates of salary due to their employment in what can never be a 'White Man's Country' are prohibitive. Government has definitely adopted the policy of employing Africans in appointments hitherto held by Europeans provided that the former are equally qualified in education, ability, and character, but progress in carrying this policy is slow owing to the scarcity of suitably qualified Africans. When, besides the need of Government, that of the European firms – mercantile, banking, and professional – is considered, it is apparent that there is a great field for the employment of well-educated Africans throughout the country.

More important still is the demand of the educated African of the existing literate classes for an education and training that will fit him to take a greater share in the development of his own land. We have not to look far for the reason. To begin with, the southern portions of the Gold Coast have been in closer contact with European civilization for a far longer period than any other of Britain's West African colonies. In the second place, our great agricultural wealth and trade are far greater in proportion to our size and population than those of almost any other tropical unit of the British Empire. Our financial resources have, in comparison

131

with our area, enabled us to cover the country with communications far more completely than has yet been found possible in countries possessing an equally productive soil and greater population. The annual increase of trade has naturally been accompanied by a steady increase of wealth until to-day we are far richer per head of the population than any of our neighbours. Now, prosperity brings a desire for the better things of life, and when this desire is heightened by the knowledge brought by the steady development of elementary education it is not surprising that there is to-day a rapidly increasing demand for better conditions of living, better sanitation, good water supplies, hospitals and dispensaries, and all the other benefits of modern civilization.

To comply with all these demands, to cope with rapidly changing conditions, Government acting by itself will make insufficient progress; its efforts must be supplemented by African enterprise. Government's duty at present is to lay the foundations of development in every direction, to organise the departmental machinery; necessary for dealing with each system, and to provide such European staff as the revenue permits; while at the same time it must prepare, organise, and bring into being a system of schools where Africans can obtain the better and higher education that will fit them to enter the various trades and professions, both in the public service and in private enterprise.

This question of providing facilities for better education and training bristles with difficulties. There is, as I have said, a universal demand by the people. To comply hastily with this demand at the present moment would be fatal, for the simple reason that we have not got an educational staff sufficiently trained to carry out the work efficiently. To do it inefficiently would be to start on the wrong road, a road along which we should have ultimately to retrace our steps; to trust the future of the race to insufficiently trained leadership in education would be far worse than having no education at all. This, then, is our immediate task – the provision of

132

well-trained teachers, instructors, and professors from among the Africans. Until we have done that we shall not be able to improve our present system of elementary education sufficiently to enable full use to be made of the secondary schools that we propose to start. Nor will the Africans themselves, who from time to time have initiated schemes for the provision of higher education by private enterprise, be able – no matter what funds they may raise – to carry out their intentions in a manner conducive to the ultimate success of their country without more and better trained teachers of their own nationality.

Higher education by itself will not solve the problem of the country. It must be accompanied by a better system of training in handicrafts, agriculture, and all those trades that go to provide for the necessities of a community; for although higher education may be the brain of a country, its productive capacity is its heart. Of what use is the brain if the heart ceases to beat? The education of the brain and the training of the hand, each accompanied by the moulding of the mind, must proceed together if success is to be sure.

The moulding of the mind! That is too important a subject to deal with here; it deserves and receives in this booklet a chapter to itself.

I am well aware of the belief held by some critics – and who has not heard it enunciated? – that the African is not capable of exercising those qualities that will be conferred on him by higher education.

Now, whatever may be my own belief – and I believe my African friends know what that is – there are two sides to every question, so I am going to examine the contention of these critics dispassionately and ask them four questions.

Firstly, have the critics ever considered that character-training is the essential factor in every branch of education but the all-essential factor in higher education has hitherto been omitted from the African's curriculum, at any rate in Africa? If they have not thought of this, may I ask them to reconsider their belief in the light of what is written in the next chapter? If they persist in their belief then they deny that a human being can rise from a lower to a higher plane of development and it does not appear to me that they receive the support of history.

Secondly, are they aware that the African races, in spite of the lack of educational facilities, of character-training, have produced men who have distinguished themselves in various walks of life, many intellectually, a number morally? America, where they have long studied the question of African education, has furnished many examples, even under the heavy handicap of 'white' opposition to after-employment. Our own African and West Indian colonies furnish others, sufficiently numerous to warrant the belief that, had character-training been in their school curriculum, success would have been wider and more complete.

Thirdly, are the critics aware of the immense field in Africa for the employment of Africans, and if so are they deliberately going to turn men who have an earnest desire for intellectual advancement – and some of whom have shown that they can benefit by it – into a race of malcontents by confining them to the subordinate work of trades and professions?

And lastly, do the critics honestly believe that we have the right to deny the African the chance of proving that his race is capable of doing what other races have done in the past? If so, they have forgotten that Britain stands where she does to-day by giving her peoples and her opponents alike a 'sporting chance'.

When all is said and done, however, it is to future generations of Africans that we must leave the task of proving that the belief of the critics of their race is wrong, of justifying the confidence placed in them by British Governments of to-day; the present generations, except in isolated instances, cannot do so – they have not had the opportunity of receiving an education and a character-training that fits them for the task.

Other critics have it that, in advocating the provision of a higher education locally for Africans, we are deliberately inviting political troubles in the Gold Coast. Surely the absolute contrary is the case. If politics are to come – and come they must if history is of any value as a guide – surely the safeguard against trouble is the local education of the many, accompanied by character-training rather than the education in Europe of a few, an education that invariably lacks character-training and that more often than not results in bad European habits replacing good African characteristics? If secondary education is not introduced to fill the gap between the English University-trained African and the semi-literate product of our primary schools, we shall be continuing our present system of providing the easy prey of the demagogue (that the late Lord Cromer warns us against).

Another criticism is, that in educating Africans to fill higher appointments in the Government service we shall be deliberately interfering with European employment in the Gold Coast. This is a short-sighted view. I have already pointed out that the development of the country necessitates an annual increase in staff. No Government in the world could afford proportionately, the immense financial burden of European salaries, passages and long furloughs that would fall on the Gold Coast if this increase was to consist of Europeans only. Apart from that, the married European with children has not and never will have a real home life in West Africa, whereas there is a great field of employment for him in the good climates of the Dominions. It will be many long years before Africans are fit to fill the higher appointments in the Government service; in the meantime there is ample room for both.

Let there be no mistake, however, about the time of transition of the African peoples from primitive to modern civilization, no false hopes about the rapidity with which they will fit themselves to stand alone. There is no short cut to success; that can only be reached by hard and steady work, by a sustained effort that will try the race as it has not been tried before. A good education and character-training are all that the Government can provide; application, work, and an honest determination to prove himself worthy are the African's share in the general task.

It has been said that we must go slow, that we must not force education on the people. With regard to the last point there is no question of forcing; one has only to see the crowd of applicants for admission surrounding the primary schools of this country at the beginning of every term. As for going slow, we are going too slow. Although it is perfectly true that the races of the Gold Coast are now in a phase through which every other race has had to pass since time immemorial, yet every century sees a quicker rate of advance made by the primitive peoples of the world. Therefore, although we may draw lessons from the past experience of other nations, it is essential that we should move faster, quicker even than the educational authorities did in the days of our youth.

Taking advantage of such lessons as can be dug out of the buried history of the Gold Coast, watching carefully for pitfalls on the road along which we are travelling to-day, striving to see through the mists of the future, we must prepare carefully the better and the higher education of the local races and their character-training. In no other way shall we fit them to absorb European civilization unhurt – and it is my belief that in no way shall we keep them permanently the loyal, worthy members of our Empire that they now are.

CHAPTER II
CHARACTER-TRAINING

No success will come – no matter how high our education or how perfect our trade training, no success will be real or will be permanent – if character is neglected. We may talk eloquently of the progress of the people being Government's first policy in this country; we may dilate on the fact that the keystone of progress is education; but all that will be idle rhetoric if we mix the materials of the keystone badly. Leave out the most important part in the material of the keystone and the arch will collapse; leave character-training out of our educational system and the progress of the African races will inevitably become a series of stumbles and falls that will leave a permanent mark on them, if it does not stop their advance altogether.

I believe that history records no single instance of a nation finally achieving greatness – attaining a permanent independent position in the world – under leaders in thought, industries, and the professions of an entirely different race. For a time it may advance along the paths that lead from a primitive to a higher state of civilization under the leadership and guidance of men of an alien race; but should it lose those leaders before it is able to stand by itself, time – it may be centuries – is lost in reaching power and independence. The races of British tropical Africa stand in that position to-day: under leaders from a Western democracy that has gradually realised its task of tutelage, they are all in varying degree emerging from primitive conditions and are pressing forward, their faces set to the goal of modern civilization. There cannot be a moment's doubt of their incapacity to-day to stand by themselves: apart from the fact that there may be Africans capable of leading in the primitive methods of native administration, there is no single race among the tropical African peoples that possesses the many leaders necessary to cope with the changing conditions that are daily wrought by the advance of European civilization – the many leaders from among

137

whom, in due course, the few may emerge who are capable of the supreme leadership.

To create these leaders is an implied part of Britain's recently self-imposed task of tutelage and development. To create them without the highest and best forms of education would be an impossibility; to think for one moment that it is possible to create them without character-training would be vain. Brain – to a leader – is of no use, is a positive danger, unless backed by force of character. Britain herself mother of the greatest Empire the world has ever seen, owes her position far more to the force of character of her sons than to their brains.

Lack of the qualities of Leadership, which in all cases involves the bearing of responsibility and in many also the power of command, is a pronounced defect among the races of the West Coast of Africa. Those citizens of the Gold Coast who have developed the qualities I have mentioned have done so by their own individual efforts and in spite of our system of education, and the majority of them only after residence in Europe. Apart from these, practically the whole of those Africans who may be said to be the leaders of thought in this country have received their higher education in Europe, where they have imbibed ideas so far in advance of the progress of the bulk of their countrymen as often to be dangerous. In many cases – again there are exceptions – it is noticeable that the young African recently returned from Europe is seriously out of touch with his countrymen. This is, I am afraid, inevitable, and will continue so long as we cannot provide in the Gold Coast a system of education in which he will receive his character-training before, and not after, he goes to Europe.

Of what I have just written I am certain. We shall fail in our self-imposed task unless we can train the character of the African; we shall not only fail in creating leaders, but we shall succeed in doing something that is far worse – making a European of him, and a bad European at that.

THE ULTIMATE OBJECTIVE

Our task bristles with difficulties. Using to the utmost our knowledge of his characteristics we have to produce a type of African who will be sufficiently imbued with European ideas to enable him to cope with the European civilization which must eventually sweep the world clear of all primitive methods of life; one who, at the same time, will remain an African, with all the best of the many fine attributes of his race. The task is, indeed, one that will have to be carried out with care and wisdom and patience; the difficulties such that Britain should be proud of having the opportunity of solving them.

Of one thing I am convinced after twenty-two years of tropical Africa: we shall never succeed if the sole place in which the African can get his higher education and his professional training is Europe. Much learning, and of the best, he can get there; character-training, none. I do not intend to enter here into the old controversy of the effect on Africans of long residence in Europe at the most impressionable period of their lives. As far as British Africa is concerned, Britain has enough to do at home in educating and training her own sons; it is in Africa, and with the aid of Africans, that the education and character-training of the African must be carried out. All those whose experience makes their opinion worth listening to, all those who have devoted any thought to the subject, are in agreement on this point, Africans and Europeans alike.

And so we arrive at one definite point anyway in our educational system, whatever the details of that may be, we must aim at giving the whole of our education locally and, where it is essential that an African should go to Europe for the final steps to enter a profession, we must arrange our system in such a manner that his absence will be reduced to the shortest possible time and the foundations of his character firmly laid before he goes.

If what I have written is right, it is evident that character-training must take a predominant place in our system of education, for the simple reason that no nation whatever can afford to omit it

139

from the curriculum of its schools. Especially is this the case when a nation is passing through a phase when the influence of home life is generally retrogressive so far as modern civilization is concerned. That this is so is inevitable; the difference will become less marked as the years pass by.

What is character-training? I confess that I have often been baffled in the attempt to define the nebulous curriculum of such a subject. We all know what we mean, but how many of us can define the word, can draw up an exact course of instruction in character-training? I think we get a good deal of help from Dr. Jesse Jones, who recently visited this country on the African Education Commission under the auspices of the Phelps-Stokes Fund. Many of us remember the deep impression made on us by the earnestness and wide views of Dr. Jesse Jones, Professor Aggrey, and their companions. The result of their travels and investigations was a book entitled Education in Africa, *a book containing a combination of idealism and practical common sense, from which we can receive, if we read with discretion, much valuable advice.*

With regard to character-training I believe that Dr. Jesse Jones hits the nail on the head. What he practically says is that there is no definite syllabus, but that whatever system we adopt, whether in infant schools, primary schools, trade schools, or secondary schools, we must endeavour to graft the simple virtues on our children. These simple virtues are perseverance, thoroughness, order, cleanliness, punctuality, thrift, temperance, self control, obedience, reliability, honesty, and respect for parents. To these I would add, if they do not include it, a correct appreciation of responsibility. As Dr. Jesse Jones says, these virtues cannot be taught out of books; they must be developed by sound habits resulting from days, weeks, and months of actual practice and repetition.

It is comparatively easy to develop the above virtues in the students of a residential school under the guidance of house-masters and instructors who have themselves had their characters developed.

THE ULTIMATE OBJECTIVE

It is far more difficult in a day school, especially when we consider the general backwardness in civilization of the student's home. We certainly do something in the day schools, but we can do nothing completely and satisfactorily until we have those boarding schools, the formation of which at present is waiting for a trained staff.

In the present phase of civilization in the Gold Coast we should have been hard put to it to find a satisfactory means of character-training if it had not been for those great movements, the Boy Scouts and the Girl Guides. Such boarding schools as we have are run on Scout and Guide lines, which contain a practical application of the principles of Christianity and citizenship that is invaluable. We have gradually introduced all these principles in our day schools, where they are accepted as the foundation of the character-training and the discipline of the school. The essence of the Boy Scout movement however, is that it is voluntary, and so difficulties have been encountered. After making experiments I believe that we have evolved a satisfactory solution. Students who enter the schools do so as 'probationer Scouts'; the conduct required from them is contained in the Scout Law; they play the Scout games and pass the Scout tests; they wear a dress consisting of the Scout shirt and shorts, but no Scout emblems or badges. In due course they become eligible to enter the troops which those teachers who are trained Scoutmasters form in every school from volunteers among the boys. By means of Scout parades orderliness, punctuality and a sense of subordination to one's seniors are impressed on the boys; by placing boys in charge of the 'Standards' or 'Sections', which correspond to the 'Troops' and 'Patrols' of the Scouts, the sense of initiative and leadership is inculcated in them. By entrusting these boy leaders with the correction of faults of unpunctuality and bad conduct a sense of responsibility is gradually formed. The system is working successfully, and has proved the great value of the application of Scout principles to a school.

Although Guggisberg drives on for another eight concentrated, short chapters, his main message has been given in the first two. Yet in the rest of the booklet he packs an amazing range of topics, a reflection of his fertile imagination, dedicated study and capacity for detail. Thus, he discusses how to raise the money for his plans, where dangers lurk on the way ahead, preventing Africans from seeking education in Europe and thus creating two classes of Africans educationally, the aims of Achimota College (which we have already discussed), the essential need for education of women and the importance of proper education and training for trades, technology and the professions. Of particular interest to this writer is the loving detail which he lavishes on Korle-Bu Hospital and its future for the training of doctors and other health professionals. Seldom, if ever, can a colonial governor have been so involved, so committed to the educational future of his subjects.

In the final chapter (X) Guggisberg highlights and enthuses over an important innovation for all the British African dependencies – the setting up of an Advisory Committee for the advancement of education on a long-term basis and not subject to the coming and going of governors.

The Committee which would sit under the Chairmanship of the Parliamentary Under-Secretary of State for the Colonies comprised two bishops, a missionary representative, experts in education, top administrators and a paid secretary. This committee was set up by the Duke of Devonshire, after he had conferred with various governors, and we can be sure that Governor Guggisberg had a major input to the negotiations. It certainly was in accord with his own ideas.

It seemed that *The Keystone* might be his final outpouring on education, but his restless spirit, paradoxically fixed on a few simple ideas, had yet another theme to explore – the education of Africans in the New World.

The Visit to North America

By introducing this interlude now, we are again jumping ahead, but it is so much a part of the educational saga that it fits here. The invitation to visit the United States came in June 1927 from Dr Jesse Jones, the Educational Director of the Phelps-Stokes Fund. He had seen Guggisberg's efforts at first hand when visiting Africa with the Commission. He invited Sir Gordon to see the many centres of special development for the American negro, particularly those with educational innovation.

The invitation must have come as a welcome relief, because by then Sir Gordon, despite his high reputation, was casting around for a suitable form of employment for his still active mind and the offer had the bonus of being completely funded by the Phelps-Stokes Trust. Although superficially busy with committee work, discussions with various influential people and fêting by his admirers, he was really at a loose end. He had by then had no offer of further employment by the Colonial Office and matters were not helped by a deterioration in his health and the breakdown of his relationship with Decima. The death of his great friend Aggrey was another sore blow.

The tour through the eastern states was a great boost to his morale. He lectured and he was received by President Coolidge and welcomed by Henry Ford and Eastman of Rochester. He had a great reception and was in his element when addressing the officers of the Canadian Military Institute. But let Sir Gordon himself speak of his American tour in the last of his books – *The Future of the Negro*.

The Future of the Negro

This small book deals with the educational future of Africans in both the New World and the Old. It was a joint effort by Sir Gordon Guggisberg and the Rev. A.G. Fraser, the first Principal of Achimota College. It is organized into three parts of roughly equal length, the first two by Guggisberg ('The Development of the American Negro' and 'The Education of the African Peoples') and the third by Fraser ('Notes on West African Education'). It was published in 1929, when Sir Gordon was Governor of British Guiana, just after his visit to Canada and the USA. As with some of his other writings, his INTRODUCTION tells us as much about himself as about his subject – particularly its last two paragraphs. We now discuss these.

Sir Gordon drew attention to the dual authorship, indicating that he had invited the contribution by A.G. Fraser in order to enhance the publication by supporting his (Guggisberg's) own theories with Fraser's knowledge and his practical experience from teaching in India, in Ceylon and at Achimota.

He recorded the gratitude of both authors to Miss Margaret Wrong of Toronto for organizing and editing bundles of rough manuscript from writers themselves 4,000 miles apart and each a similar distance from her. His last remark was that he hoped that her refusal to be regarded as a co-author was due to modesty and not to avoid implied association with himself and Fraser.

This Introduction was intialled only by F.G.G. on 10 May 1927 (by then he was in Georgetown, British Guiana).

One gets the feeling that Fraser and Miss Wrong needed some persuasion to undertake their parts of the work and that Guggisberg, now far from well, had lost a little of his confidence and power. Nor does it seem derogatory or insulting to the memory of the great man to suggest that these two paragraphs betray a paradoxical hint of humility and arrogance (for Fraser's initials are not appended to the Introduction! This may not just have been due to their distance apart.).

PART 1: 'The Development of the American Negro' is in many ways the better part of Guggisberg's contribution to the book, for it explores new ground, and not just geographically. In fact one feels a lifting of his spirit and enthusiasm as he warms to his task. He examines the migration of African Americans northwards and their struggle against white supremacy continuing after nominal emancipation, but he accepts the difficulty that successive American governments had to improve the lot of so many under-privileged people, not forgetting the problems of white Southerners ruined by the Civil War. But there is no point in straying from Guggisberg's main theme and main reason for visiting the USA – to learn about the education of the Negro in the American setting. He finds that, although the coloured population lag far behind in education, particularly at university level, there have been worthwhile, though modest, advances. He pinpoints four main reasons for the improvement in the situation.

First, the creation of endowment funds by generous and public-spirited white millionaires to promote education, health and research across the whole racial spectrum. These funds were well managed and usually disbursed to groups or individuals who were already helping themselves. He particularly mentions John D. Rockefeller and Julius R. Rosenwald (the owner of the Sears-Roebuck Mail Order Company).

Second, the fact of negroes helping themselves. The greatest individual contribution towards education with an underlying Christian ethos and a concentration on practical training in farming and economics was made by Booker T. Washington (1851 to 1915). He had been born into slavery, but, on liberation, worked for his own education on the fields of the Hampton Institute in Virginia and then founded two small schools in shacks at Tuskegee, Alabama. He was partly funded by Rosenwald to develop six new schools. He left a wonderful legacy and a unique memorial, for by the time of Guggisberg's pilgrimage the Booker T. Washington schools had spread through the United States and multiplied to about four thousand, with approximately ten thousand teachers and half a million Negro children! Booker T. Washington's ability, actions and attitudes did a great deal to improve race relations.

Third, the education of coloured people was enhanced by the Inter-racial Commission, a group of about a hundred leading white and coloured men and women who promoted mutual goodwill and co-operation in a wide range of civic affairs and stimulated teaching and research notably at the University of North Carolina.

Fourth, the US Congress was taking an increasing interest in and financial support for universal education, matching state investment with an equal amount of federal money.

Sir Gordon was obviously moved by his whole experience of meeting the American cousins of the Africans whom he had devotedly steered towards prosperity, health, knowledge and the development of skills and character.

There is a great deal more detail in this part of the book, but by now the reader will have received its main message.

PART II: 'The Education of the African Peoples' contains material already considered by Sir Gordon, e.g. in *The Keystone* and so it will not be discussed in detail. However, there is a sequence of a few pages (pp. 67-70) which conveys much of his aims for the future of the inhabitants of the Gold Coast in economic, political and religious terms. This will now be considered.

Guggisberg appeared concerned that the world in general found it hard to accept that his type of imperialism was a trusteeship, not a process of oppression and exploitation. He emphasized that this principle of trusteeship was accepted by and was being implemented by British colonial administrations in Africa other than the Gold Coast, being delayed exceptionally only because of local circumstances. He did admit, however, that this virtue had a reward in terms of the prosperity of those places where the trusteeship was most conscientiously carried out, as in the Gold Coast. He then went on to discuss two ways in which enlightened policy had led to favourable developments in that colony.

First he described the expansion of the cocoa trade from tiny beginnings to a then current annual production of almost a quarter of a million tons. As discussed in Chapter XXI, this was due primarily to African initiative and the faithful, skilful work of numerous African peasant farmers. Such lucrative trade brought prosperity to these independent workers and indeed to the whole country. The customs export levy on cocoa was used to finance the development of education, the building of Takoradi harbour, expansion of railways, the construction of health-care facilities and the improvement of water supplies and other public works – in short for the benefit of the natives. Guggisberg kept the involvement of overseas companies and administration in the trade to a minimum.

He next turned to the development of democratic government. In this he believed in evolution, not revolution. He felt it would be inappropriate in a country 90 per cent illiterate to introduce a full European system involving ballot box and one man, one vote. Instead he had decided the early steps towards democracy by the dual system of tribal rule through provincial councils and through municipal government with representation of both on the Legislative Council, which also had official and unofficial European members. These moves will be discussed also in Chapter XXVII.

He emphasized that many of the local laws, by which the Africans governed themselves for many generations, have as their basis the sanctions of traditional religions; so too have many of the rules of their social life. He was worried that many excellent native institutions had been lost by a too radical conversion to Christianity.

Prominent among such sanctions are those relating to sex, puberty, initiation rites and marriage – some repugnant to Europeans, but, nevertheless, codes of conduct established through the centuries. He maintained that something had to be done to compensate for the loss of such customs; and that would require the earnest co-operation of missionaries, anthropologists and the medical profession to devise a scheme for the teaching of practical hygiene.

Guggisberg could see how the clashing of ancient native culture with the (for them) newly engrafted Christian religion had led to damage to both. He thought that such a clash rendered much missionary effort ineffectual. On the other hand he was in no doubt that what he called practical Christianity, as shown in the teachings and life of Jesus Christ, gave a sound basis for successful and civilized living. That aspect of Christianity was of infinitely greater importance than dogma or ritual, and had guided the development of the greatest civilization in history. His wish was for the African peoples to attain such a high degree of development along their own racial lines. (On a lighter note, one aspect of African culture which he could not abide was African music; it is ironic that this would so far seem to constitute their greatest impact on the culture of the developed world!)

One can only marvel at Sir Gordon's wonderful insight into the problems of a developing nation and his ability to handle so much detail and so many ideas, but we learned that he could do it even from his 'youth', in his writing of *The Shop* and *Modern Warfare*.

PART III: Notes on West African Education by A.G. Fraser
What can one say about this section of the book? It was the contribution of an experienced and innovative educator, but although Mr Fraser had decided views on his subject, his style is more tentative than that of his enthusiastic amateur co-author.

He deprecated the tendency in government schools to concentrate on a weak form of so-called vocational education, which used English to the exclusion of local languages and succeeded only in partly training a small number of young men for menial clerical tasks.[1]

He was also highly critical of the fact that at least four times as many boys as girls were being educated. Such an imbalance did not help the next generation, led to men being bored with their wives and tended to increase immorality.

Mission schools had a better record than government schools in the teaching of girls and in using the schools to train the young in the practicalities of living; and they were cheaper than government schools, particularly as regards salaries and administration. He praised Sister Magdalen's Catholic school and the now renowned Mary Slessor

---

1. Current author's footnote – that opinion appears to ignore English as the main language of modern knowledge and its common usage by peoples of so many disparate tongues.

Memorial School under the United Free Church of Scotland (both in Calabar).

As might be expected he thought that the Bible was the best book for the teaching of English, vastly superior to lightweight school readers and rich in lessons for living.

He pointed out that many teachers, as they grew older, became stale and dull and that initial training and refresher courses should be more dynamic and less detailed than they were. Rote learning at all levels should be reduced.

Fraser was sure that the school had its greatest value as a part of the community, taking an interest in everyday problems and using these as the subject matter for the education of the young by developing their ability to solve problems in general.

He was strongly critical too of the fact that government Education and Health Departments had no official links and did not wish to promote a joint health education programme.

Fraser finished his section by emphasizing how children require heroes to stimulate them to real effort. He ended with a question. Who was a greater hero than Christ?

Concluding Remarks on Education

Without embarking on a long and potentially boring appraisal, it is not possible to present a structured critique of the five-course banquet to which the reader has been invited and by which, hopefully, entertained, interested and enlightened.

Guggisberg was a man with a mission in education, although he was unorthodox in some of his views e.g. that primary education was more important than maternal influence. Yet he had the good sense and good fortune to secure the services of two outstanding professionals, Aggrey and Fraser, to launch his greatest project, Achimota College.

Under this inspired, dedicated and inspiring triumvirate education became alive.

Chapter XXIII

THE UNSURPASSED TECHNOCRAT: THE UNWILLING POLITICIAN

Guggisberg was in no doubt about his real métier, which he defined only a few days after arriving as Governor. Thus, as has already been recorded: *'I am an Engineer, sent here to superintend the construction of a broad Highway of progress along which the races of the Gold Coast may advance ...'*

There has been much discussion about Guggisberg's performance as a Governor; how lacking he was in accepted training for such an appointment and in political subtleties. Yet these speculations are largely irrelevant in the face of his material attainments and their felicitous consequences for the development and prosperity of the Colony. By concentrating on his main objectives – transport, health and education – he delivered what was needed at that hour. He had the technical understanding to handle these problems more successfully than could have been done by any other governor of his time.

As a soldier, he was trained to obey commands and to issue commands, and, in his rôle as Governor, he had ultimate local authority. He was thus fortunate in that, although he had to listen to debates, including criticisms of his plans and actions, it was *his* decision as to how much attention to pay to them. However, his long-term aim for the Colony was for gradual progress towards a form of independence, at a pace to be decided by the pace of educational and material achievements and as a unique unit within the British family of nations. Thus, it was during his rule, that the first tentative steps towards democratizing the Colony were taken; steps about which there was much prolonged controversy and enforced compromise.

The main difficulty was that any political initiative had to attempt to reconcile the old feudal system of paramount chiefs, lesser chiefs, village headmen and their subjects in an as yet predominantly rural population, with the rise of an educated middle class in the larger coastal towns. Guggisberg respected the small, but vociferous elite of intellectuals, but his affection was more for the chiefs and the mutually loyal regimes they represented, despite their sometimes considerable inadequacies.

In general it was Guggisberg who set the pace in construction and educational programmes, but in most political matters he tended to function in a more reactive manner, responding, sometimes with great skill, to problems as they arose. A few of these will now be discussed.

Chapter XXIV

THE RETURN OF KING PREMPEH
TO KUMASI

After a series of armed struggles between the Ashanti tribes and the British, King Prempeh, the paramount chief or Asantehene was banished in 1896 to the Seychelle Islands with several of his close relatives. Further hostilities followed, including the siege of Kumasi Fort, where the Governor, Sir Frederick Hodgson and Lady Hodgson were trapped. (Remember her escape in a bullet-proof hammock!) After that situation had been resolved, Ashanti moved on to a slow improvement in security and a better relationship with the British, mainly under the able guidance of Mr (later Sir) Francis Fuller, the Chief Commissioner.

However, there were still problems, because the removal of the Asantehene created a power vacuum and led to rival factions developing and to the weakening of the tribal system. It was natural, too, that there should be disappointment and resentment about the arbitrary continuance of the exile, despite petitions for the return of the King. Ashanti support for Britain in the First World War created a much more favourable climate for ending the unsatisfactory situation.

Guggisberg had great sympathy for the exile, growing old

thousands of miles from home; and his mother and brother had died there. The Governor felt that Prempeh and his people had suffered enough. Yet he did not wish to stir up political unrest and upset his urgent programme of development.

But, only at his second Legislative Council meeting, in November 1919, he was called upon to grasp the nettle, by having to consider this Resolution:

> *That in the opinion of this Council, the time has arrived when the question of the release of ex-King Prempeh from his exile in the Seychelle Islands should receive the favourable consideration of His Majesty's Government, and we most respectfully and humbly pray that Royal clemency may be exercised in his favour.*

The Resolution was eloquently moved and seconded by Nana Ofori Atta, Omanhene (Paramount Chief) of Akim Abuakwa and Mr. E.J.P. Brown, one of the African intellectuals. Not one of the African members of the Council was an Ashanti, but all supported the motion, stressing the peace and prosperity of Ashanti, loyalty in the Great War and the conversion of Prempeh to Christianity. None of the Europeans spoke.

In this, one of his major tests of political skill, Guggisberg acted very wisely. Clearly sympathetic to the motion, but wary of too sudden a move, he gained a breathing space by indicating that a decision should not be taken until the retiral (now imminent) of the highly successful and popular Chief Commissioner, Sir Francis Fuller; but he promised to bring notice of the debate to the attention of the Secretary of State.

He did keep his promise, but moved slowly on the process of clearing the way for Prempeh's return home. Political moves in London and work by Fuller's successor, Harper, on the proposed Native Jurisdiction Ordinance for Ashanti facilitated the matter. (The latter clarified the positions of Government and the Divisional Chiefs, strengthening the latter.) His rebus gestis, Prempeh was allowed to return as a private citizen in 1924. Two years later, after a petition by the Divisional Chiefs that he be reinstated as their Omanhene, this wish was granted by the Secretary of State. It all seemed an unusually cautious process, but Guggisberg, pressed upon by so many different facts and factions, had to be sure to do the right thing; and he did!

Chapter XXV

STATUS AND SALARY IN GOVERNMENT SERVICE

For the individual educated African both these topics caused much concern. The major aims of the Governor, with the support of the native leaders, were being successfully pursued. Yet the small, but growing African professional classes were unhappy about career prospects. The situation had not always been so, for in the nineteenth century Africans of outstanding ability, such as George Ferguson, the surveyor and government agent, were promoted to important positions. But in the first two decades of the twentieth century there was an unhappy reversal of this development, partly as a result of the increasing complexity of administration,[1] partly to give more career opportunities to Europeans. In fact, by the time Clifford was appointed Governor, promotion of administrators, judges and medical officers was largely restricted to Europeans. To his credit, Clifford took the initial steps towards rectifying this, but, not surprisingly, it was Guggisberg who advocated a stronger drive towards Africanization of professional posts, aiming for over 50 per cent to be held by Africans. It made

---

1. There was even a move to make appointments as *District* Commissioners dependent on having an official legal qualification as solicitor or barrister.

good economic sense, because long furloughs, expensive sea passages and overseas allowances were a greater financial burden. (Readers wishing to study these developments in detail should read *A Political History of Ghana, 1850 to 1928*, by David Kimble, 1963.)

Not only did Guggisberg increase the range of posts open to Africans, he also supported demands for increased salaries for civil servants from the lowest grades upwards to keep in line with inflation. There is nothing unique about this aspect of Guggisberg's administration, but it is of interest that the main resistance to such expenditure came from Winston Churchill who had replaced Milner as Secretary of State for the Colonies.

Throughout these transactions on status and salaries Guggisberg was very careful to keep the Legislative Council fully informed. For this he was openly praised by J.E. Casely Hayford, which was somewhat unexpected because he tended to be a rather critical member of the Council and, as we shall see in another political controversy, soon to be considered, was sometimes awkward.

Finally, in relation to official appointments, it is appalling that African doctors, fully qualified in Britain, were being denied senior appointments within the service. Until Clifford and Guggisberg forced the issue, they were kept in junior grades.

Chapter XXVI

THE NATIONAL CONGRESS
OF BRITISH WEST AFRICA

Like the problem over ex-King Prempeh, the activities of this organization erupted on Guggisberg early in his Governorship. Although it originated mainly in the Gold Coast, it was complicated by its involving all four British West African colonies – the Gambia, Sierra Leone, the Gold Coast and Nigeria. Its chief organizer was J.E. Casely Hayford, who, as the reader will recall, was a leading African member of the Legislative Council and a barrister of no mean ability. Members were mainly intellectuals from the coastal towns, without a significant input from the chiefs. A Conference was planned to be held in Accra in March 1920, but Clifford had only a superficial inkling of what was afoot and Guggisberg took up office quite uninformed of these plans. It did appear that he had had no briefing from Clifford on the matter.

This group of intellectuals were intent on greater representation in colonial government and on promoting a union of the four colonies, but, perhaps surprisingly in view of the ability and experience of Casely Hayford, they had not discussed their plans with the administration, with the chiefs or with the Aborigines' Rights Protection Society (ARPS), the main watchdog for the rights of the Africans. The ARPS had its main support from the chiefs of the Western Region of the Gold Coast. So, before going on to discuss how Casely Hayford and his friends eventually failed in their mission, let us cast back to the origins of the ARPS which was founded at Cape Coast in 1897.

The Society was formed as a response to an ill-conceived Ordinance by which it was planned 'to vest Waste Lands, Forest Lands and Minerals in the Queen', the main thrust of which was that lands which were not identified as belonging to an individual, a tribe or a chief would automatically fall to the Crown. This was intolerable, for the Gold Coast was a protectorate, not a possession; it led to the founding of the ARPS and an outright rejection of the Ordinance. An acceptable Ordinance relating to land tenure and mining concessions followed a few years later and the surveying required to implement this later bill is what first brought Guggisberg to the Gold Coast!

The aborted ordinance was out of character with most of the handling of native affairs, for the British authorities were usually assiduous in the prevention of exploitation. For example, Legislative Council reports just before Guggisberg's Governorship contained references to the Master and Servant Ordinance, an old measure to prevent any possibility of recrudescence of slavery. For instance, the Elder-Dempster Shipping Company had to obtain the specific authority of the Legislative Council to engage the services of six men from the Gold Coast as stewards on their liners plying between West Africa and Liverpool.

Let us now return to the activities of the National

Congress of British West Africa. Casely Hayford was the inspiration and driving force. He was the first person to see the potential unity of the four English-speaking West African lands. On a personal level he had close relatives in Sierra Leone. In 1913 he wrote the stirring words: 'One touch of nature has made all West Africa kin. The common danger to our ancestral lands has made us one – one in danger, one in safety. United we stand divided we fall ... United West Africa ... shall take her true part among the nations of the earth.'

Fine-sounding words! But from the start, even attempts to form a society to promote the idea led to Casely Hayford's quarrelling with his associates. Significantly, too, an editorial in February 1915 in the newspaper *Gold Coast Nation* poured cold water on the concept of a common purpose among such a disparate and geographically separate group of countries. (A sound judgement in view of what has happened in Africa in recent years.)

Yet Casely Hayford's persistent enthusiasm eventually led to the first West African Conference which took place in Accra in March 1920.

Although the slight to the new Governor was not obviously intended or on a personal basis, the group lost the possibility of an ally in some of their aims. The irony of the situation was that their ambitions for Western style democracy were no greater than Guggisberg would have been pleased to support. He did not offer direct criticism, but he did ask the question (without attempting to answer it) as to whom these professionals claimed to represent.

(They were in fact a small group who wished to promote

their own intellectual oligarchy to replace the tribal system. They had no relevant electorate except in the larger coastal towns.)

However, Guggisberg, had he had prior warning, would have attended their conference to hear their views at first hand. But by the time he knew of it, he was already committed to a tour of other parts of the Colony and decided not to let down those he had promised to visit.

Then Casely Hayford committed the cardinal sin of going behind the Governor's back by leading a delegation to London to petition Viscount Milner and attempt to have an audience with King George V.

This played right into Guggisberg's hands. As soon as they were on board ship bound for Liverpool, he sent a telegram to the Secretary of State, pointing out the weakness of their case and their underhand move. The delegation were *not* received, either by Milner or the King; their cause was lost. Guggisberg's initial reaction was of anger; his official response was cool, but devastating. (Yet he and Casely Hayford were later able to function together in the Legislative Council.) Clifford's rage with the Nigerians on the Delegation knew no bounds. (It was a pity that he and Guggisberg, with this mutual problem did not become reconciled.)

Thus Guggisberg carried through another test of political skill with his reputation again enhanced. The national congress of British West Africa had wasted a potential friendship, e.g. in relation to plans they had for a University to serve all four colonies; they also erred in quarrelling with Nana Ofori Atta, the most influential of the paramount

163

chiefs. (This is a very condensed version of a highly complex story; it can be studied in detail in Kimble's *Political History of Ghana.*)

Chapter XXVII

FIRST STEPS ON THE ROAD TO DEMOCRACY AND INDEPENDENCE

When a Governor, Guggisberg functioned as an autocrat. Yet he looked on his régime as an interim state of affairs, a trusteeship which would eventually lead to democracy and independence. We have already studied his own views on the matter in Part II of *The Future of the Negro* – 'The Education of the African Peoples'. He was sure that full Western-style democracy had to wait until there was a much more widely educated and prosperous electorate. (Conditions which could well have been made a prerequisite for democratic development in general!) But he was not content to let things drift, and, as he himself recorded, he was able, after several years of negotiations, to make an offer, which was reluctantly accepted, of a compromise – a dual development in democracy – using tribal system and municipal government. The chiefs were organized into Provincial Councils, with enhanced representation on the Legislative Council, and the intellectuals of the coastal towns became part of democratic municipal government, again with representation on the Legislative Council.

This arrangement was acceptable in the late 1920s; not surprisingly, it was rejected later in the face of more strident nationalism and the demand for 'one man one vote'. Yet it kept the wheels of government turning. The system was a necessary compromise. Its adoption was greatly facilitated by the now unsurpassed reputation of Sir Gordon and the material progress he had brought to the Colony. In fact, it is not too exaggerated to say that he was not just the Governor of the Gold Coast, he had become the embodiment of the Gold Coast.[1]

But this moment of eulogy is marred by a sad downside: the fact that such a great leader, a man with a genius for handling difficult planning and political affairs, an accepted paternal figure in his adopted country, had no home life, in fact never really had a home of his own. Thus in the last page of his wonderful biography, Wraith, obviously deeply moved, records how Sir Gordon headed his last letter to his friends as from Bexhill-on-Sea, but on the top right-hand corner wrote:

Permanent address:
The Army and Navy Club,
Pall Mall, S.W. 1.

This shorter biography will end on a happier note, but we must still look briefly at the downside of Guggisberg's life: his two unhappy marriages. His public service was a superb success, his private life a failure.

---

1. In his relationship with the Africans, his innate skills were honed by the anthropological researches of Captain R.S. Rattray.

Chapter XXVIII

PRIVATE RELATIONSHIPS

None of Guggisberg's biographers have been able to account for the disastrous personal relationships of a man who was so successful in his handling of staff (military and civilian, European and African) and of his colonial subjects. To some extent the tolerance of his subordinates may have been enhanced by his own obvious dedication, unsparing personal efforts, disarming frankness and friendliness and the feeling that they were on a ship which was on a successful voyage. Yet Oman, the director of education for the Gold Coast, must have been at the point of exploding in the face of so much interference with his department, and Guggisberg's relationship with Fraser was a stormy one, for both had hot tempers. So all was not as happy as might have seemed from superficial examination.

This writer has sought the reaction of members of the opposite sex of different ages to some of the facts about his two marriages and *all* react unfavourably, some quite strongly. Let us look at a few of these facts.

The first marriage, to Ethel Emily, was a hasty one, an elopement from Singapore to Ceylon when she was only seventeen. Presumably, as the daughter of a senior army officer, she had led a sheltered life, with no domestic chores or responsibilities, particularly in the East. Then, only so quickly, the romantic honeymoon on the exotic island was followed by three pregnancies in rapid succession, the first sadly leading to the death of their infant daughter.

The young lady had little idea of running a home, particularly on the limited income of a junior officer and almost certainly did not appreciate being lectured to by her mathematically precise husband on how to balance the books.

Then Guggisberg did an amazing thing: he got his mother to take charge of the household. That was the last straw; Ethel eloped again – this time with an Anglican parson; Guggisberg was left with two young motherless daughters; he divorced their mother – a little more later about the daughters.

The second marriage was the second also for Decima. With her theatrical connections and his flair for always being immaculately dressed, even for informal occasions, they became part of a smart set about town in Edwardian London, but, on the other hand, she joined him enthusiastically in his surveying expeditions in the African bush, thoroughly enjoying the adventure and their contacts with the natives. Yet, even in these days, one detects that he was readily annoyed by Decima.

During the Great War, they went their separate and highly successful ways and, as already discussed he would not have become Governor without her help. She had the personality and energy to be an ideal wife for a high official, except that she was a prima donna and could not play second to anyone, even a Governor.

A highlight of her career as Governor's wife was her organizing of and playing hostess at the Gold Coast stand at the British Empire Exhibition at Wembley in 1924. In this she had the able co-operation of her husband's old friend Colonel Levey.

Yet they continued to get on each other's nerves and this erupted into a blazing row in public in 1925, during the visit of Princess Marie Louise to the Gold Coast. The reception party was assembled and, as the royal visitor approached, Decima stepped forward in front of Gordon to greet her – an unpardonable violation of protocol for anyone to go before the King's representative! Gordon grabbed Decima and pushed her behind him amid a heated verbal exchange.

It was sad that, as his great assignment was coming to an end and doubts about his faith, his finances, his future employment and his health were bearing hard upon him, he was losing any possibility of a reconciliation with Decima. There was no real bond between them. Decima was particularly nasty to Miss Corry of Yateley Hall, the lady with whom Guggisberg's daughters made their home, accusing her of coming between them (Gordon and Decima) and breaking up their (non-existent) home! So great had become the rift between them that, after his death, she refused to give Wraith any help with his book.

But let us not continue to wallow in that swamp.

Yateley Hall, on the edge of Army Territory, in north Hampshire, not far from the cricket pitch of the Royal Military College, Sandhurst, was indeed a haven of relaxation for Sir Gordon, where, even when restricted in mobility by poor circulation in his legs, he could enjoy sketching, painting in watercolours and, especially, carpentry. There, too, after he had finally left the 'Coast', he was able to entertain Aggrey on what was to be his last journey to America and the durable Fraser, about to return to Achimota.

Chapter XXIX

THE GOVERNOR'S ANNUAL ADDRESS TO THE LEGISLATIVE COUNCIL OF THE GOLD COAST, ESTIMATES SESSION, MARCH 1927

This was not just the annual event, it was Guggisberg's final report on his stewardship of the Colony for eight years.

The Report, of over 300 pages, ran to 347 itemized paragraphs. As usual, every detail of events, achievements, and activities of departments and of individual officers was recorded. No one was forgotten and no one would be allowed to forget.

Para 1 dealt with trade and revenue: since the War trade had trebled in tonnage and quadrupled its value; revenue almost trebled.

Para 2 dealt with the main events of 1926-7.

(i) The coming into force of the new Constitution granting electoral representation on the Legislative Council for the first time to the people of the country.

(ii) The formation of Provincial Councils of Paramount Chiefs.

(iii) The opening of Achimota.

(iv) The passing of the Forestry Ordinance.

(v) The entry of the first steamer into Takoradi harbour.

(vi) The visit of the Parliamentary Under-Secretary of State for the Colonies (Mr Ormsby-Gore).

(vii) The opening of the Gold Coast Commercial Intelligence Bureau in London.

The Governor also recorded how he had already urged the Paramount Chiefs to have their possible successors properly educated.

Obviously it would require a whole book to comment on all the 347 paragraphs, but only a few of particular interest will be mentioned.

Para 273 dealt with rises in municipal rates (e.g. 3 per cent to 5 per cent in Cape Coast) to pay for improvements in hygiene.

Para 276 dealt with the retiral of the Comptroller of Customs, Captain J.M. Reid and changes consequent to that. This was a financially important post because it held responsibility for the collection of the main revenue, viz. duty on cocoa exports. (The writer has a personal interest in the late Captain Reid as Captain Reid's youngest daughter is a friend.)

Para 286 dealt with the Geological Survey, obviously of great importance as it was under the direction of a high-ranking official, Sir A.E. Kitson. Two items investigated were of particular value in view of later developments: the assessment of the dry-season flow of the Black and White Volta Rivers and their potential for hydro-electric power and the testing of bauxite deposits. (First hints of Akosombo Dam and Power Station and Tema Aluminium Smelter.)

Para 288, on the Gold Coast Regiment, contained two typical 'Guggisgergian' comments:

> *I congratulate the Commanding Officer on the fact that neither at the camp, nor on the march to and from it, was there one single complaint by civilians against the behaviour of the troops* [Remember the Southern Nigeria Survey]; *and I should like to compliment Bandmaster T.A. Medhurst on the proficiency of the Band of the Regiment.* [Old soldiers never die!]

The Report was a fitting farewell from a man whose mind still retained and organized every detail.

Chapter XXX

BRITISH GUIANA

Guggisberg was Governor of British Guiana for only eight months (November 1928 to July 1929). The assignment was not quite a poison chalice, but it was fraught with difficulties that would have fully stretched a younger, fitter man. In the three months between being appointed and reaching the colony, he made the expected intensive study of the serious problems of this small territory and, with his still incisive intelligence, identified several which required action. The foremost was lack of population and he set in train steps to rectify this by promoting immigration from the West Indies and from the East, thus leading to a racial mix of Afro-Caribbean, (East) Indian and Chinese settlers. This also required the allocation of viable agricultural units. The Administration was complicated and chaotic and had to be properly organized. Finances were in a precarious state and the main cash crop, sugar cane, could not have survived without the protection of 'imperial preference'.

With so many defects to be corrected Guggisberg seemed the ideal choice for Governor. Such was his reputation that his coming was welcomed with Messianic expectations.

The manner of his arrival in Georgetown was dramatic. The ship bringing him docked precisely on time and only the ship's officers and crew could be seen (all passengers other than the Governor's party being confined to their cabins). There was 'a hush of expectation'; then the great man appeared on the bridge, tall and gaunt, in full regalia, followed by his ADC (a retired Rear Admiral) and his Private Secretary (a retired Brigadier-General), both in full-dress uniform. The record-sized crowd went wild with excitement.

As he drove slowly through the mob, some broke the police cordon to shake him by the hand and one woman shouted, 'Our Father, our Saviour has come!' Supreme theatre!

But, sadly, the struggle to raise the fortunes of Guiana met with little success. Guggisberg's plans were basically sound, but the honeymoon was soon over. As his physical powers waned, he became more and more dictatorial and dismissive of criticism. There was no rapport. Eventually he became so unwell that he had to leave the Colony. He maintained that he would return, but whether he really believed it is doubtful. His departure could not have been a greater contrast to his arrival. He gave a farewell address at an informal meeting of the Legislative Council and was then driven in an ambulance past a few silent onlookers to his ship. It was all so sad, such a change from his African successes that there seems no point in elaborating the tragedy.

Chapter XXXI

PAST THE POINT OF NO RETURN

Guggisberg became too ill to resume his duties in Guiana, reluctantly admitted defeat and officially retired on 15 January 1930. He had spent several distressing and uncomfortable months in various nursing homes being investigated and treated for amoebic dysentery which had involved his liver and he was also suffering from chronic heart failure and arterial disease of the legs, which limited his ability to walk – a sorry state for a former athlete. It was thought that his circulatory problems were due to the drug emetin which was used to treat the amoebic infection, but there may also have been another factor – heavy smoking. Oddly enough a clue is given in a cartoon of Sir Gordon in the magazine *Nigerian Field* which shows him with an elegant cigarette holder clenched between his teeth. But this observation is not for the gratification of the more strident members of the anti-smoking lobby, important though their cause has become. For in Guggisberg's day the dangers of cigarettes were not understood and men who served in the First World War found cigarettes, like the rum ration, to give a transient relief from the insane torture of the trenches. These heroes, voluntary or conscripted, were thus helped to keep going, as the song reminds us:

Caricature of Sir Gordon Guggisberg. He was elegantly dressed.
Note the cane and the cigarette holder! Both may have been
related to the poor circulation in his legs.
Reproduced with the 'blessing' of the Editor of the *Nigerian Field*.

Pack up your troubles in your old kit-bag,
And smile, smile, smile!
While there's a lucifer to light your fag,
Smile boys, that's the style!

In short, Guggisberg may well have died from a combination of service on the Western Front and service in West Africa. After his death his great friend the paramount chief Nana Sir Ofori Atta wrote: 'Sir Gordon died for Africa. What is more important and harder for him, he lived for Africa.'

As well as having to endure increasing physical incapacity and the anguish of a leader, previously fully occupied and successful, but now without prospects of suitable employment, Sir Gordon had financial worries. He had an army pension of about £500 a year, but, because he had not served the minimum of ten years as a governor, he did not qualify for a governor's pension (£700 a year). His illness was proving costly and he was particularly worried about supporting his daughters.

From a London nursing home, he was driven by road to his ultimate earthly destination, a modest boarding house (No. 27, Cantelupe Road) in Bexhill-on-Sea. There he spent the last three months of his life in a room without a view, but well supported by friends (some of whom had previously retired to Bexhill). Two doctors attended him, Dr Webb a local practitioner, and Dr Cecil Le Fanu (the latter who had served in the Gold Coast apparently functioned more as a friend than a physician).

His only sight of the sea was when his daughter Rowena took him out one day in a bath chair.

A different view of Sir Gordon Guggisberg's grave from that
shown in the Frontispiece. Photographed by John Hooper of
Eastbourne. Mr Hooper has captured with admirable skill the
stature of Sir Gordon (6 feet 4 inches) and the solid granite
wall round the grave is appropriate to his early appointment
as an Instructor in Fortification.

At times he was, not surprisingly, low in spirits,
and flagging in faith, but towards the end he derived
peace of mind from a book he had been given by Fraser –
Sin, Suffering and Sorrow by Bishop Walter Carey of
Bloemfontein – and in his daydreams he planned to spend
the rest of his life either as a mission teacher in Africa or
travelling by barge along the canals in the English
countryside, preaching to the people, but, as Wraith
remarked, it was not clear whether he wanted faith in Christ
or faith in the Empire. (Apparently he had made real plans

179

to fit out a barge, but, after his death, his daughters put a stop to the work.)

His death was peaceful, his funeral modest for such an eminent man, but dramatized at the end by Decima's laying a wreath on the coffin as it was lowered into the grave.

His worldly wealth, only £1,934.6.6, was left to his two daughters. The Gold Coast Government voted modest pensions to his widow and daughters (later continued by the Ghana Government).

For four years the grave was an unmarked mound of earth. His family could not afford a suitable stone and no one else in Britain did anything about it.

Then Nana Sir Ofori Atta came to pay his final respects to his friend. He was shocked and angered by the unmarked grave and organized the erection of a memorial worthy of the great man. This is how our story began, but unlike Wraith's otherwise splendid biography, we must not end here.

Chapter XXXII

THE EPILOGUE

The evil that men do lives after them;
The good is oft interred with their bones.

Julius Caesar, Act III, Scene II –
Mark Antony's speech at Caesar's funeral.

The plays of William Shakespeare contain much worldly wisdom, often ringing true, but this quotation is far off the mark in Guggisberg's case. Thus, by sustained and almost superhuman efforts, he guided the Gold Coast Colony to an enlightened and potentially prosperous future. Perhaps, if he had been diverted from his main objectives of improving transport, health and education and had become too embroiled in political controversy, he would not in the end have been so revered. Remember, too, that his army career and pioneering surveys rendered great service to his country, his comrades and the West African colonies. It was only when he was a spent force that he was unable to follow through his plans for the resurrection of British Guiana.

R.E. Wraith's biography, *Guggisberg*, is a fund of information about our hero and conveys an admirable degree of understanding of such an enigmatic personality: in turn modest and arrogant; dedicated to duty and good causes yet sport-loving and a great club man; attractive to women but irascible and high-handed with them; a stickler for protocol and appearing in full regalia, yet happy relaxing with African villagers over a cup of tea or an informal cricket match.

The present writer is uncomfortable with only a few aspects of Wraith's discussions. First, it is surprising that he spends time on some of the criticism directed by others against Guggisberg's support for the chiefs and thus for the indirect type of colonial rule, so strongly developed by Lugard in Northern Nigeria; by implication suggesting that Guggisberg should have given full support to Casely Hayford and the minority of intellectuals who wanted to overthrow the traditional régime. Guggisberg himself explains why in *The Future of the Negro*. And surely there would have been chaos had that happened prematurely.

Another surprise is that Wraith took the trouble to discuss the idea that Guggisberg's development of transport was to facilitate trade for the benefit of British capitalists. This, again, is untenable in the face of Guggisberg's 'Preliminary Report of Transportation in the Gold Coast Colony'. Thus: *'The only further comment that appears necessary is that the natives of the country are the principal shareholders in this matter of trade.'* To reject this is to accuse the Governor of gross duplicity. (However this document may well have been denied to Wraith by the Fifty-Year Rule). From a personal point of view, Guggisberg's life savings of £1,934.6.6 were not quite on the scale of Rhodes's personal fortune!

The other slight confusion in Wraith's biography is the variable message given as to Guggisberg's Christian faith.

182

However, in such a large and intensively researched book, these are minor criticisms.

Wraith devotes a whole Chapter to what he calls 'The Springs of Action' – what made Guggisberg tick? This is one of the many unanswered questions about such a complex character – and there are also questions still to be asked. For example the origins of the Guggisberg family are still obscure and the generally accepted story is not yet documented. (The present writer has so far failed to obtain information from Switzerland.) Decima introduced an element of doubt by maintaining that Guggisberg was German, not Swiss. The possible Jewish ancestry does appear to have modified Guggisberg's attitude to the oppressed.

He was sensitive about his name and one wonders why, when he was still a young child, he was not given his stepfather's surname – Dennis? Would history have been different if he had simply been Gordon Dennis? But enough of these speculations about what might have been! Let us finally look at his influence on others during life and after death.

Mention has already been made of a lady whose father was Comptroller of Customs under Guggisberg. The father of another lady whom the writer met first at Kumasi was Guggisberg's chief clerk in the Royal Engineers in France. The message from both these ladies was of the power of his personality and his total commitment to his tasks.

There is no doubting the importance of Takoradi harbour e.g. one wonders if Churchill ever acknowledged its significance for the staging of aircraft for the Middle East during the Second World War. Planes in crates were unloaded and assembled for the flight to Egypt. Perhaps the only weakness in Guggisberg's development of transport was in not realizing that road haulage would become more important than the railways and one of the few unfinished schemes for transport was that, mainly for financial reasons, the northern extension of the railway was never pursued.

We have already followed some of the consequences of the building of Korle-Bu Hospital, but a small vignette about Achimota is not inappropriate. An English lady, now in dental practice in the east of Scotland, spent much of her early life in Ghana. She tells of watching the then youthful Jerry Rawlings, a fellow-pupil at Achimota, drilling a squad of cadets outside the College. It must surely gladden the heart of Guggisberg that a product of his great school is now in charge!

Guggisberg was a superb practitioner of the art of public relations; so much so that the enormous input of others to his material successes tends to be ignored. But, in a sense, he was like one of the great trees of the tropical rainforest. He required the others to attain his immense stature. Thus, without the lobbying of Decima, Viscount Milner would never have appointed him as Governor and he required Milner's support to handle the Colonial Office. The various groups on the Legislative Council, although sometimes critical, did, on the whole, give him strong support, particularly Nana Sir Ofori Atta. Aggrey and Fraser were essential to the success of Achimota. Nor must we forget Sir Hugh Clifford – highly critical, but the man who had already initiated some of the schemes brought to fruition by Sir Gordon.

Guggisberg was unique, but he was not alone!

Bibliography

Books written by F.G. Guggisberg
1. *The Shop: The Story of the Royal Military Academy* (1900)
   Written by Captain F.G. Guggisberg.
   Published by Cassell and Co, London.
2. *Modern Warfare* (1903)
   Written by 'Ubique' – nom-de-plume of Captain F.G. Guggisberg.
   Published by Thomas Nelson and Sons, London
   (Reprinted during First World War, 1914 to 1918).
3. *We Two in West Africa* (1909)
   Written by Decima Moore and Major F.G. Guggisberg.
   Published by William Heinemann, London.
4. *Handbook of the Southern Nigeria Survey and Textbook of Topographical Surveying in Tropical Africa* (1911)
   Written by Major F.G. Guggisberg.
   Published by the Southern Nigeria Survey Office, London.
5. *The Keystone* (1924)
   Written by Brigadier-General Sir Gordon Guggisberg.
   Published by Simpkin, Marshall, Hamilton, Kent and Co, Ltd, London, EC4.
6. *The Future of the Negro* (1929)
   Written by Brigadier-General Sir Gordon Guggisberg and A.G. Fraser MA.
   Published by the Student Christian Movement Press, London, WC1.

Publications specifically about Sir Gordon Guggisberg

1. *In Memoirs: Royal Engineers' Journal*
Brigadier-General Sir Frederick Gordon Guggisberg
KCMG CMG DSO RE (March 1931) (Plus small later
correction), pp. 134 to 140, by 'GGW'.
2. *Obituary in Who Was Who* (1929 to 1940)
p. 565.
3. *Obituary in Dictionary of National Biography* (1922 to 1930)
Sir Frederick Gordon Guggisberg (1869 to 1930), pp. 368
to 369, by Lord (Sydney) Olivier.
Edited by J.R.H. Weaver. Oxford University Press.
4. *Guggisberg* (1967)
by R.E. Wraith. Oxford University Press, (the only major
biography to date).
5. *'Guggisberg: a Biographical Sketch'*
by Robert Addo-Fening. In Golden Jubilee Souvenir,
Korle-Bu Hospital, 1923 to 1973.

Documents Examined in Public Record Office (PRO) Kew
Papers about the Gold Coast Colony, mainly between 1916
and 1930. Especially from Original Correspondence – CO96
and Sessional Papers – CO98 including Departmental and
Special Reports. Those papers copied verbatim are quoted in
Acknowledgements.

Publications Related to the Start of the First World War
1. *Atlas of World History: Volume Two* (1979)
Original written by Herman Kinder and Werner
Hilgemann.
Translated from German to English by Ernest A. Meize.
Maps by Harold and Ruth Bukor.

Original published by Deutscher Taschenbuch Verlag GmbH and Co, KG.
English edition by Penguin Reference Books.

2. *Before the War* (1920)
Written by Viscount Haldane.
Published by Cassell and Co, London.

3. *The War Behind The War* (1914 to 1918)
A history of the Political and Civilian Fronts (1939).
Written by Frank P. Chambers.
Published by Faber and Faber, London.

4. *Ludendorff*
The Tragedy of a Military Mind.
Written by Karl Tschappik.
Translated by W.H. Johnston.
English version published in 1932 by Greenwood Press, Westport, Conn., USA.

Books on the History of the Gold Coast Colony and Ghana

1. *Ghana – The Road to Independence*
F.M. Bourret (1960).
Oxford University Press.

2. *West Africa under Colonial Rule*
M. Crowder (1968).
Hutchinson, London.

3. *A Political History of Ghana*
David Kimble (1963).
Clarendon Press, Oxford.
(Some idea of the thoroughness of the *magnum opus* is conveyed in the author's final remark on page 562 '... and the pressing need for further study'. But his work was for a doctorate!)

4. *The Cambridge History of Africa* Volume 7 (1986)
   Edited by A.D. Roberts.
   Cambridge University Press.
5. *A History of Ghana*
   by W.E.F. Ward 1966 (Sixth Impression)
   (Originally published in 1948 as *A History of the Gold Coast*).
   George Allen and Unwin Ltd, London.

Miscellaneous

1. *Nine Great Africans*
   by Sir Rex Niven (1964).
   Roy Publishers Inc, New York.
   (The 9th was Dr J.E.K. Aggrey.)
2. *The Goldon Stool*
   by Edwin W. Smith (1926).
   Holborn Publishing House, London EC1.
   (A key to the history of Ashanti.)
3. *The D'Oyly Carte Opera Company, 1875 to 1982*
   by Tony Joseph (1994).
   Bunthorne Books, Bristol.
4. *Dictionary of National Biography*
   Obituaries on Viscount Milner, Sir Matthew Nathan and
   Sir Hugh Clifford.
5. *Who Was Who*
   Obituaries on Rev. Dr A.G. Fraser and Sir (Alexander)
   Ransford Slater).
6. *British Medical Journal* (see Chapter XX)
   (a) 1927: Obituary on Professor Adrian Stokes.
   (b) 1928: Obituaries on Professor Hideyo Noguchi and Dr
   W.A. (Bill) Young.

BIBLIOGRAPHY

Paper by Dr Edward Hindle on a Yellow Fever Vaccine.
(c) 1995: Aug 19 pp. 492 to 494.
'The Hard Boiled Saint: Selwyn-Clarke in Hong Kong'
by Mervyn Horder.